Sit & Solve

CHESS PROBLEMS

BURT HOCHBERG

Sterling Publishing Co., Inc.
New York

Library of Congress Cataloging-in-Publication Data Available

4 6 8 10 9 7 5

Published by Sterling Publishing Co., Inc.
387 Park Avenue South, New York, NY 10016
Copyright © 2004 by Burt Hochberg
Distributed in Canada by Sterling Publishing
℅ Canadian Manda Group, 165 Dufferin Street,
Toronto, Ontario, Canada M6K 3H6
Distributed in Great Britain by Chrysalis Books Group PLC
The Chrysalis Building, Bramley Road, London W10 6SP, England
Distributed in Australia by Capricorn Link (Australia) Pty. Ltd.
P.O. Box 704, Windsor, NSW 2756, Australia

Sterling ISBN 1-4027-1450-5
For information about custom editions, special sales, premium and
corporate purchases, please contact Sterling Special Sales
Department at 800-805-5489 or specialsales@sterlingpub.com

CONTENTS

INTRODUCTION & How to Solve

A direct-mate problem stipulates that White moves first and mates Black in a specified number of moves, no matter what Black plays. In a mate-in-two problem, White moves first, then Black, then White mates on his second move. The stipulation is inviolable: mate must be accomplished in exactly two moves, no more, no fewer.

Here is a collection of
"abbreviated" two-move chess problems
with White's first move already played. The rest of
the solution–the Black defenses and the mating moves that
refute them–is for you to find. The stipulation for every
problem in this book is:

Black to move, then White mates in one.

Knowing that White must mate on the next move, your job
is to find each of Black's relevant defenses–moves that attempt
to avert or avoid the mate–and the White moves that refute
them. I emphasize relevant. Not every conceivable Black move
is relevant to the solution. For example, in No. 1, White threatens
2 Rb5#. Black's bishop has nothing to do with that threat,
so none of its possible moves are listed.

One way to start solving these puzzles is to
locate the Black king and find a

mating move by White.
Then see what moves by Black meet
that threat. That's not the whole story, of course.
Every move you make for Black will be met by a White
mate—not necessarily the mate you've defended against but
an unexpected move from elsewhere on the board. This new
mate has been made possible by the defense you played against the
original threat! The real fun of solving these puzzles is seeing how
ingeniously their composers have accounted for every detail.

My thanks to Peter Gordon, my editor
at Sterling Publishing, who was quite taken with
this new type of puzzle, which he called Mate in 1½.

Thanks also to my everlastingly
patient wife, Carol.

Burt Hochberg

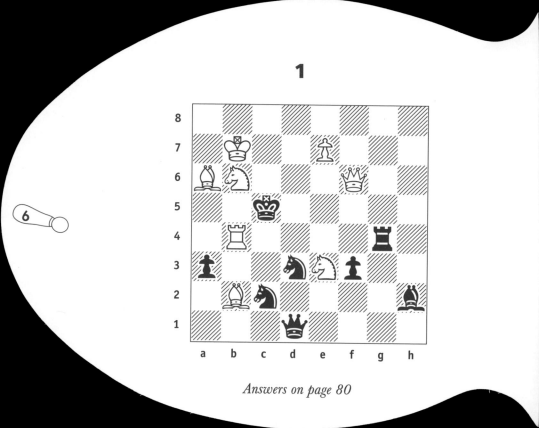

1

Answers on page 80

2

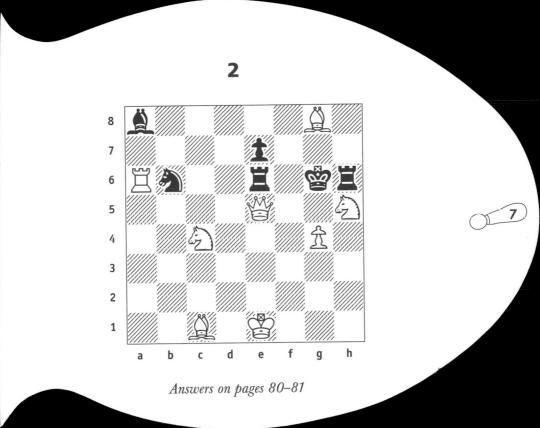

7

Answers on pages 80–81

3

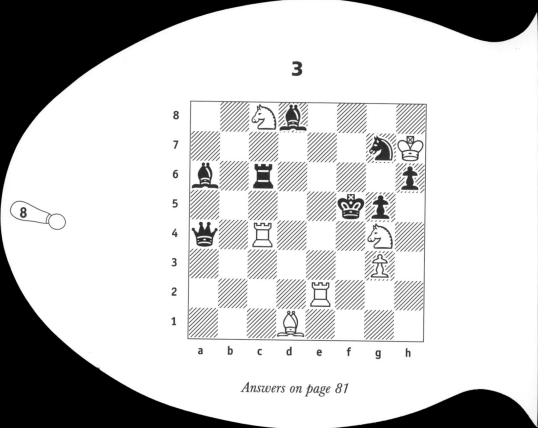

Answers on page 81

4

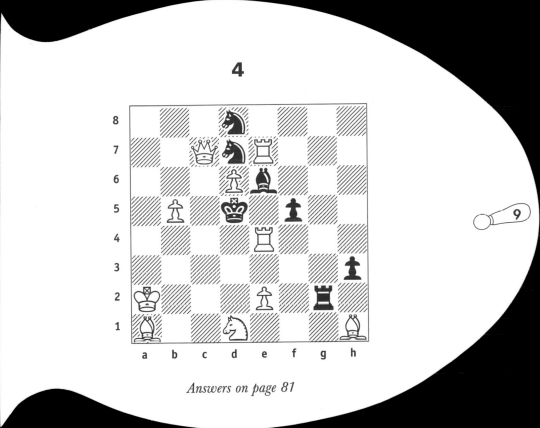

Answers on page 81

9

5

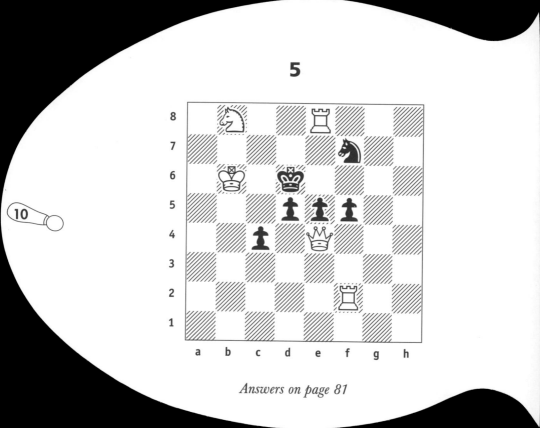

Answers on page 81

10

6

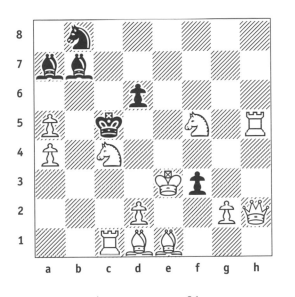

Answers on page 81

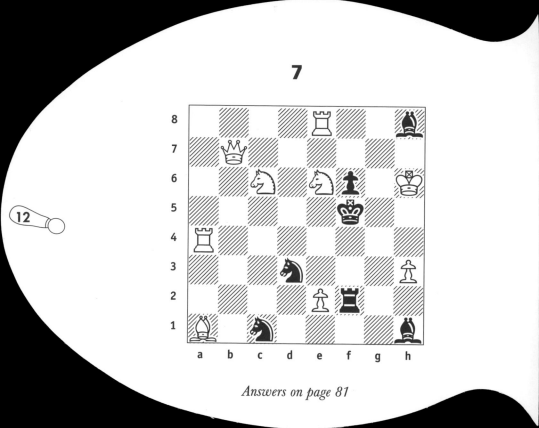

Answers on page 81

8

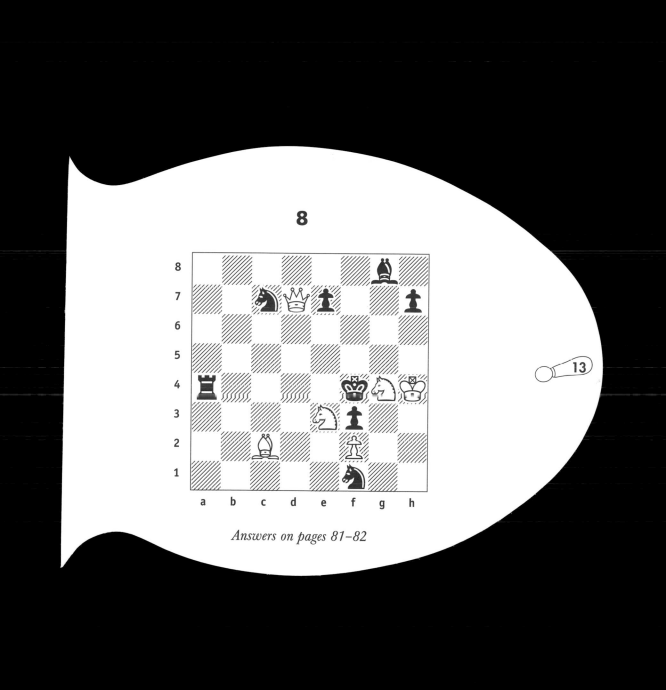

Answers on pages 81–82

13

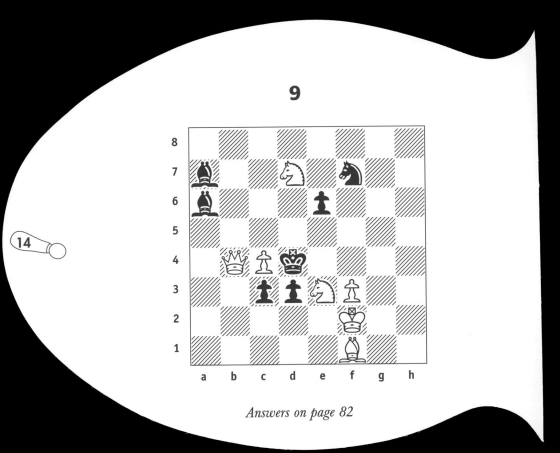

14

Answers on page 82

10

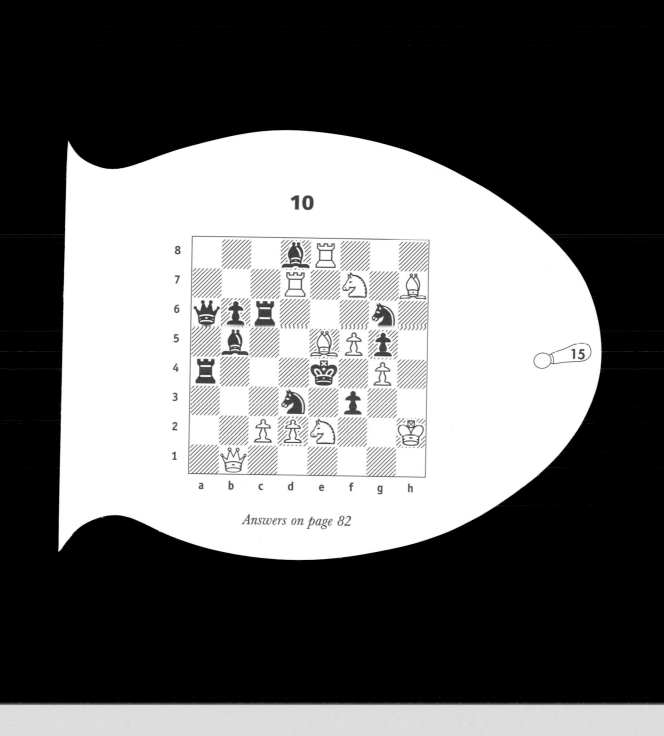

Answers on page 82

15

11

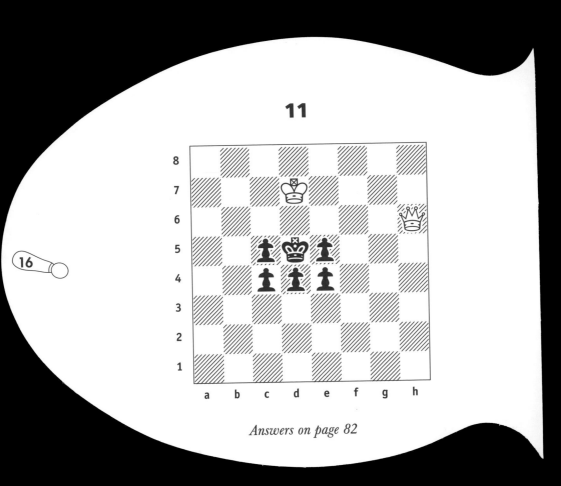

Answers on page 82

12

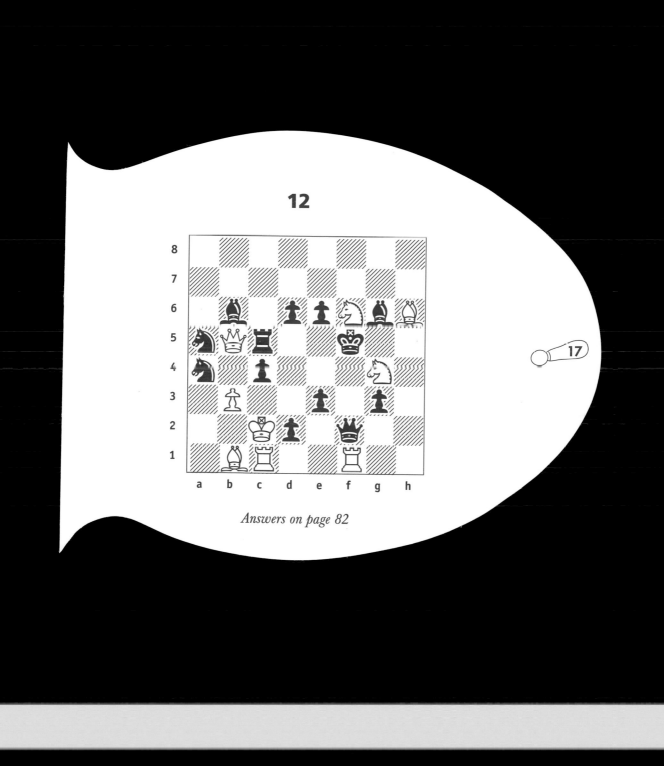

Answers on page 82

13

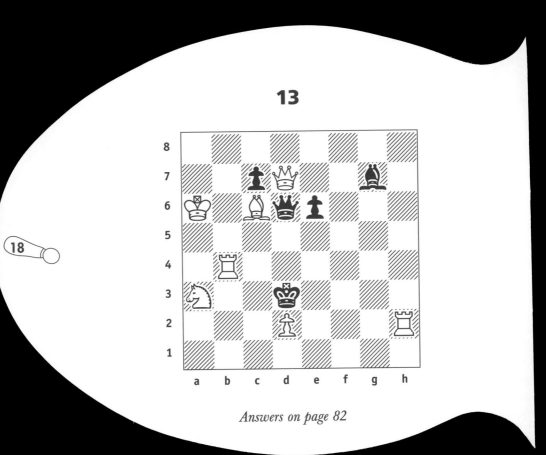

Answers on page 82

18

14

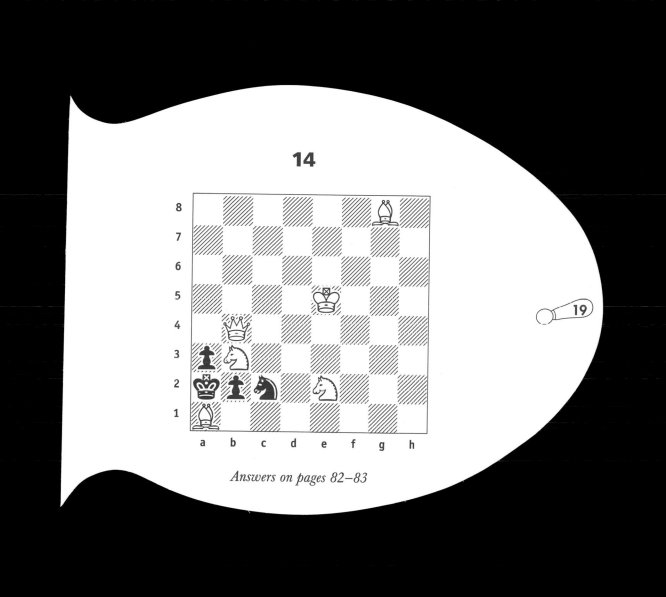

19

Answers on pages 82–83

15

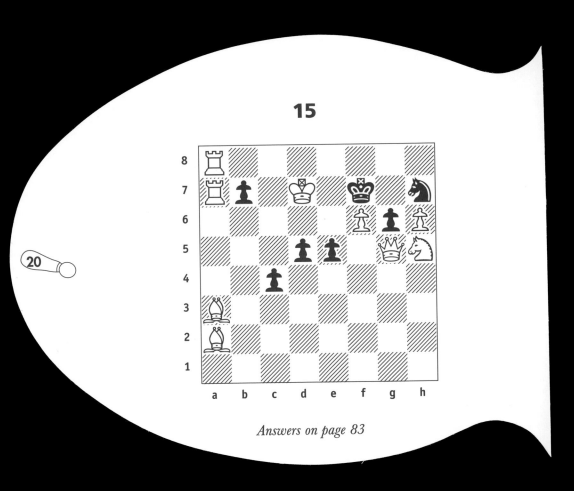

20

Answers on page 83

16

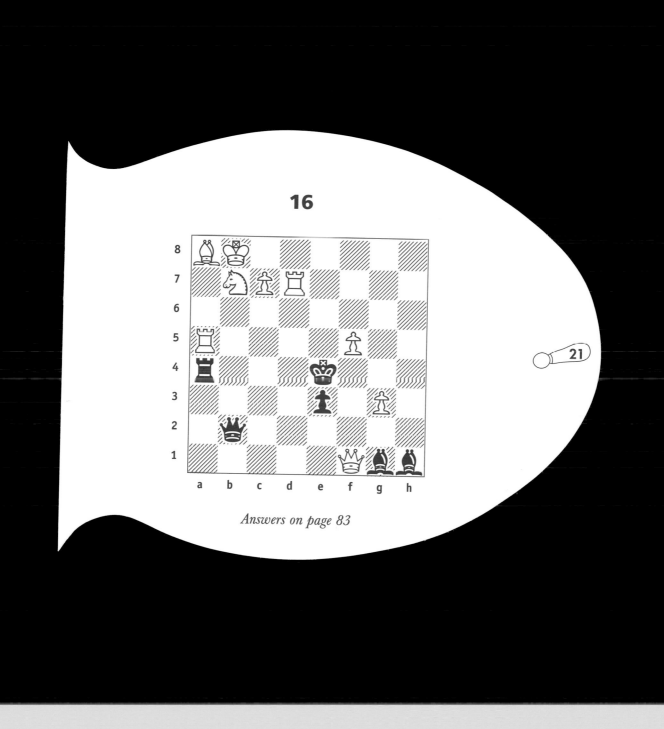

Answers on page 83

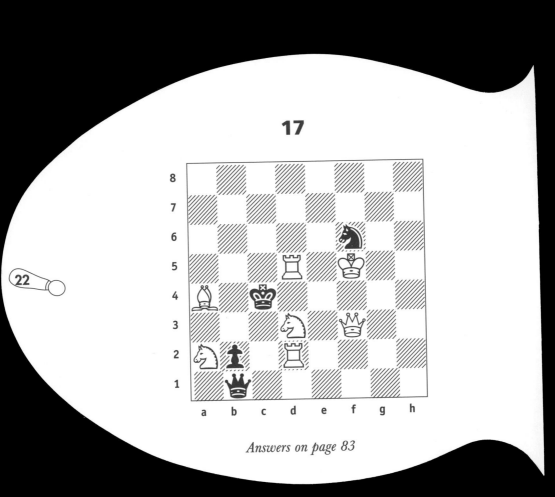

Answers on page 83

18

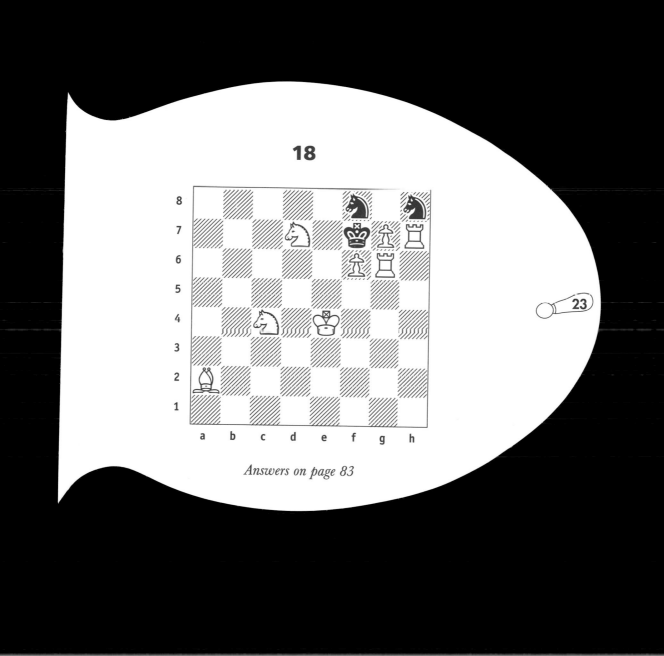

Answers on page 83

23

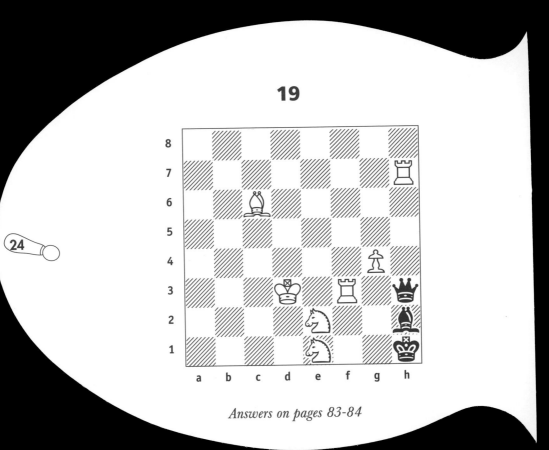

Answers on pages 83-84

20

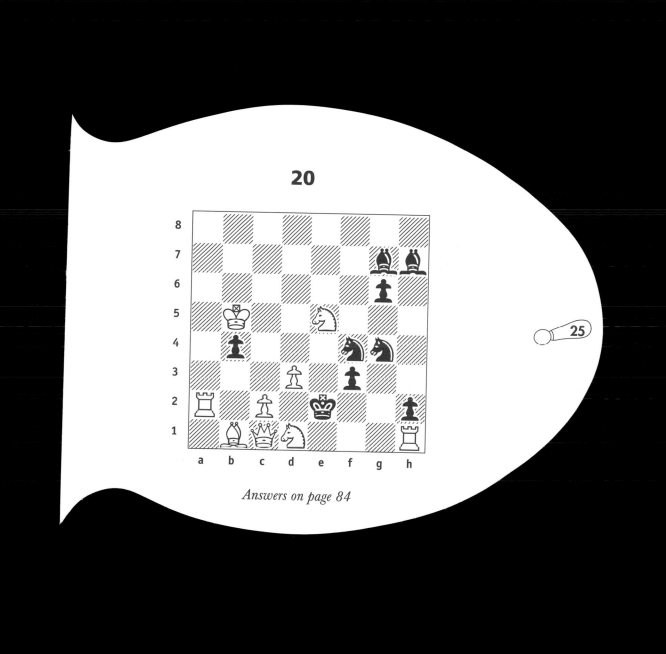

Answers on page 84

25

21

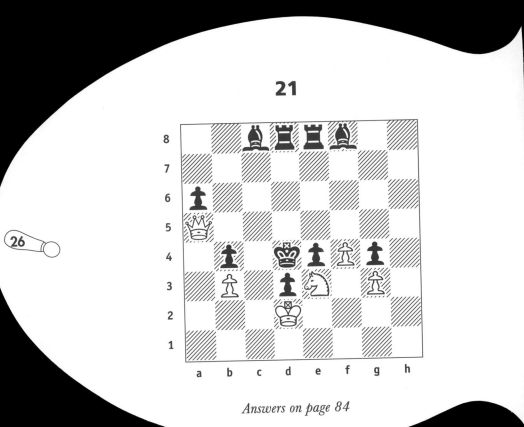

Answers on page 84

26

22

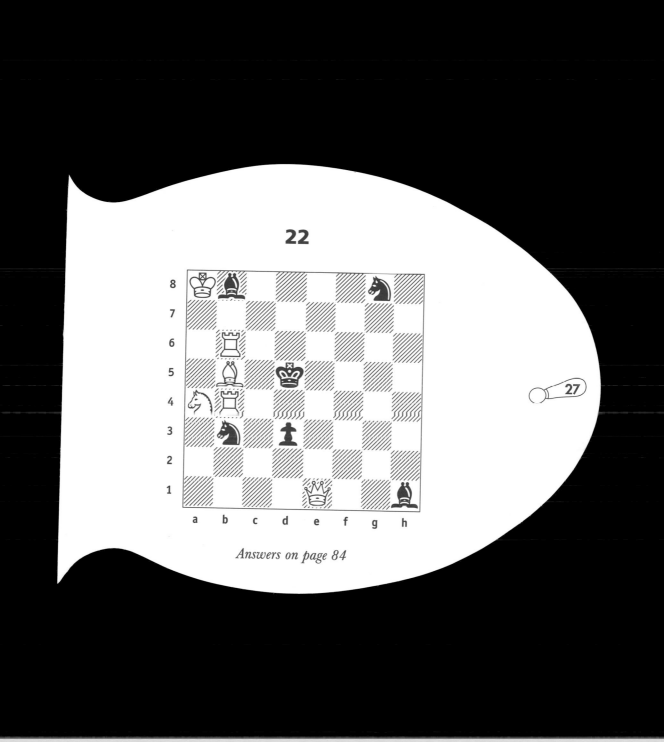

Answers on page 84

27

23

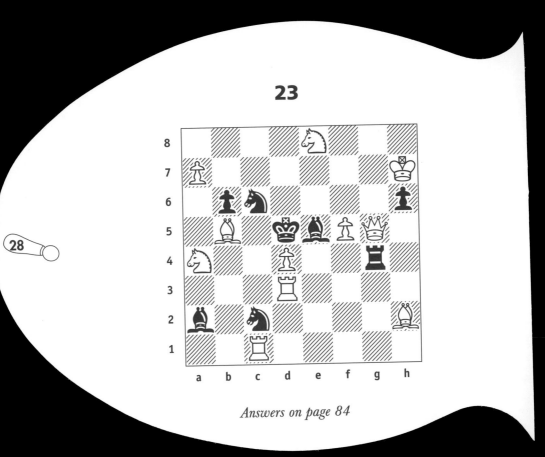

Answers on page 84

28

24

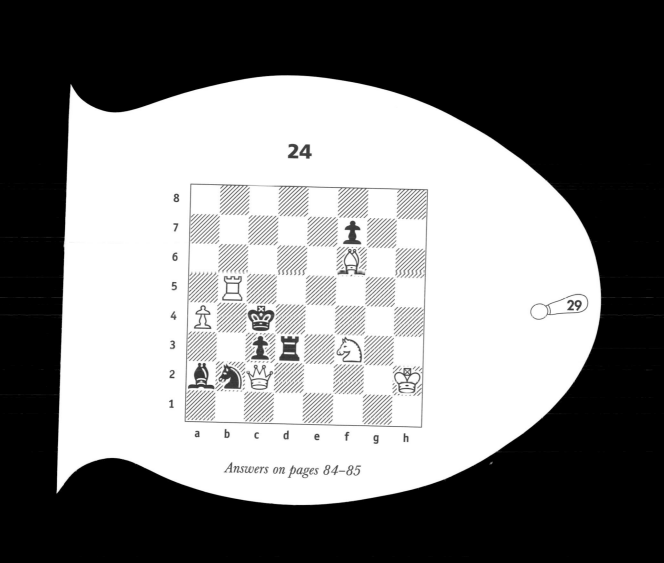

29

Answers on pages 84–85

25

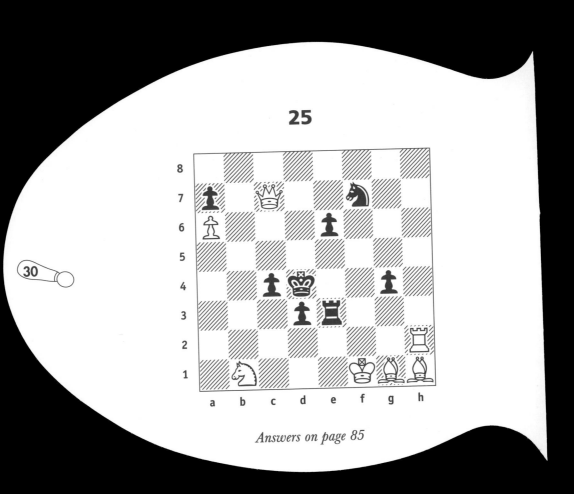

Answers on page 85

26

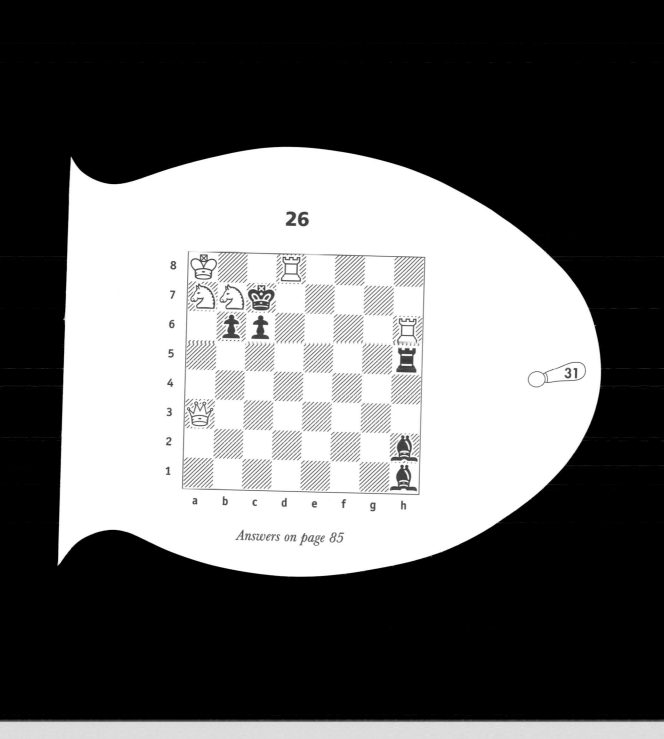

31

Answers on page 85

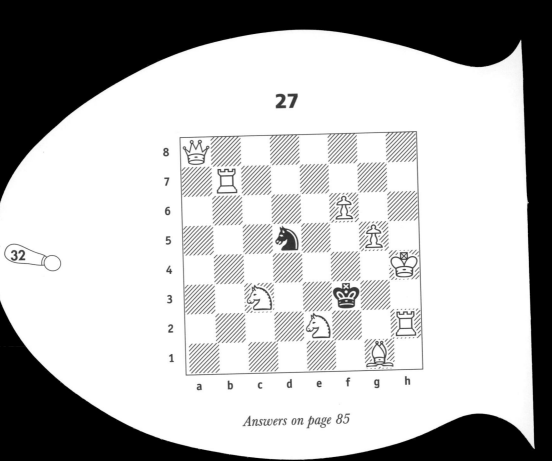

Answers on page 85

32

28

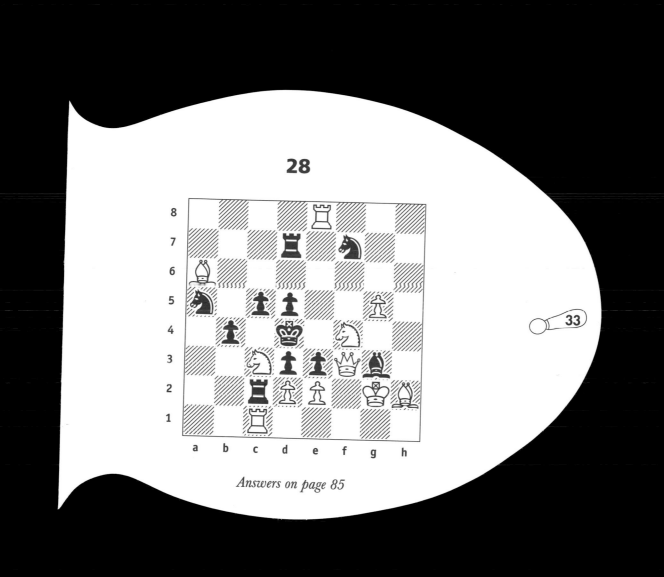

Answers on page 85

33

29

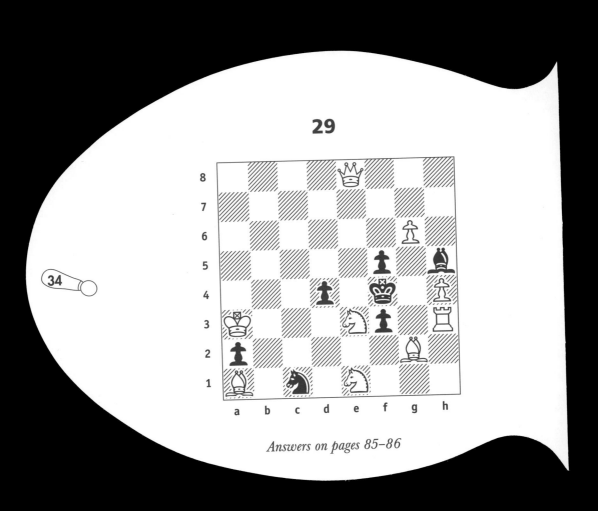

Answers on pages 85–86

30

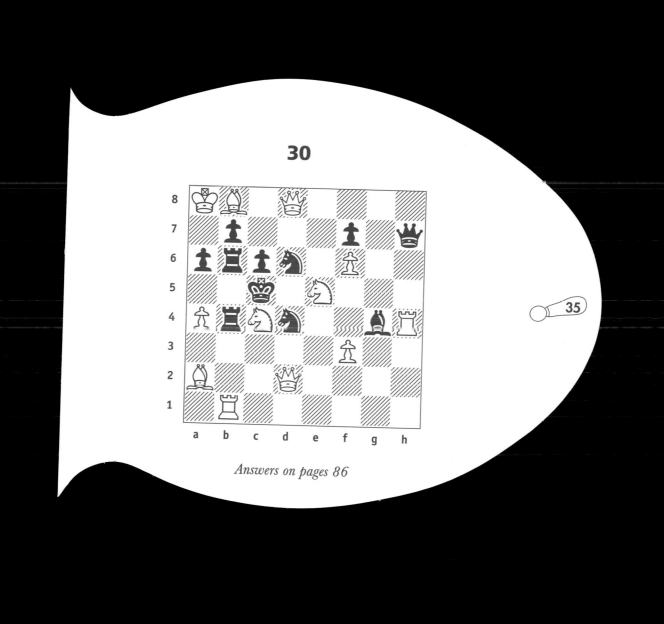

35

Answers on pages 86

31

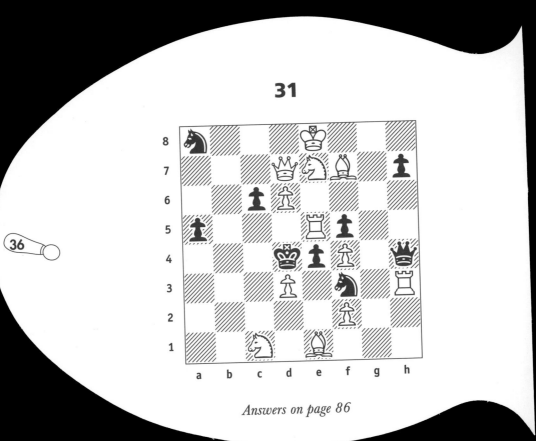

Answers on page 86

32

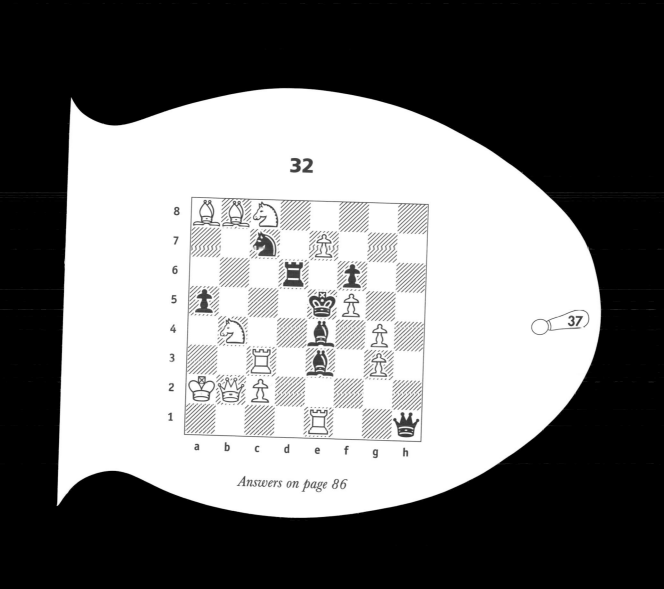

Answers on page 86

37

33

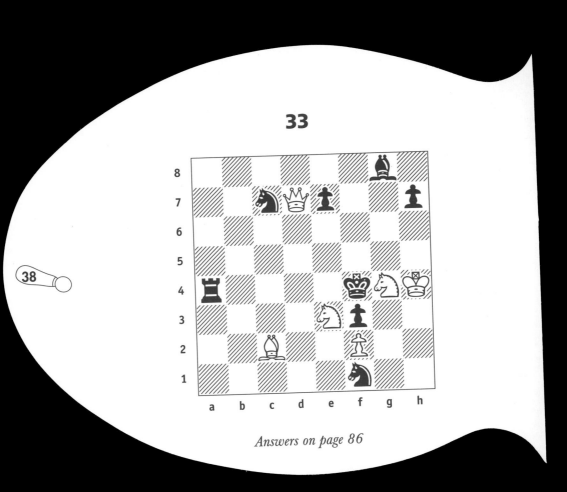

Answers on page 86

34

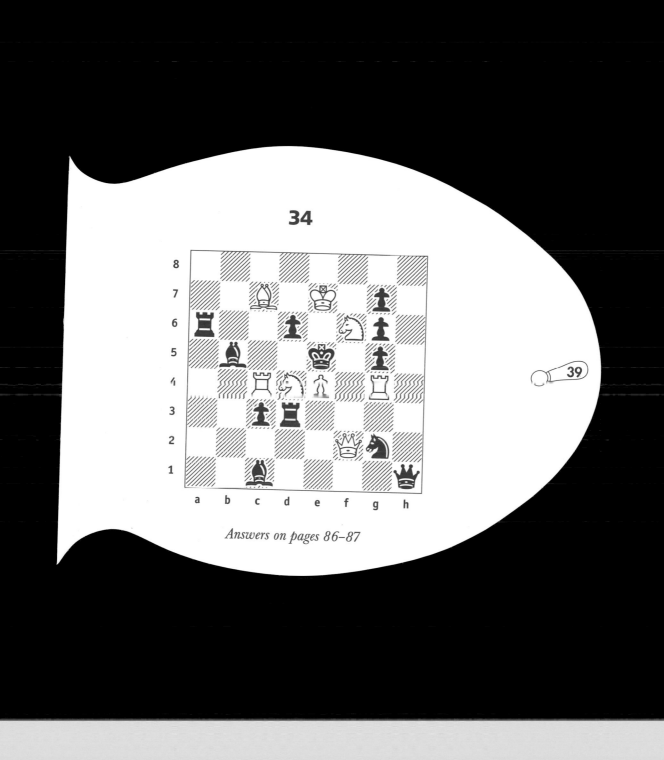

Answers on pages 86–87

39

35

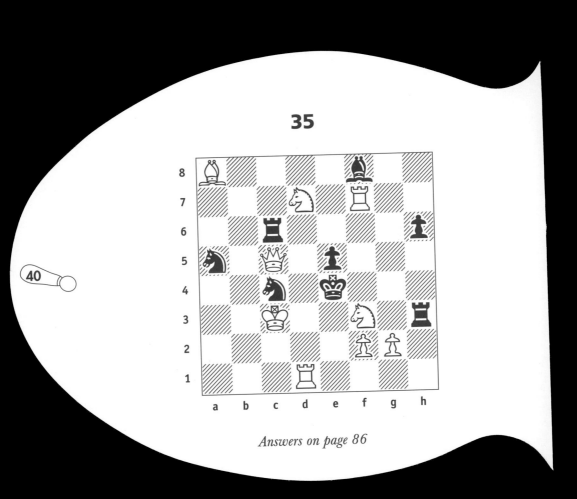

Answers on page 86

40

36

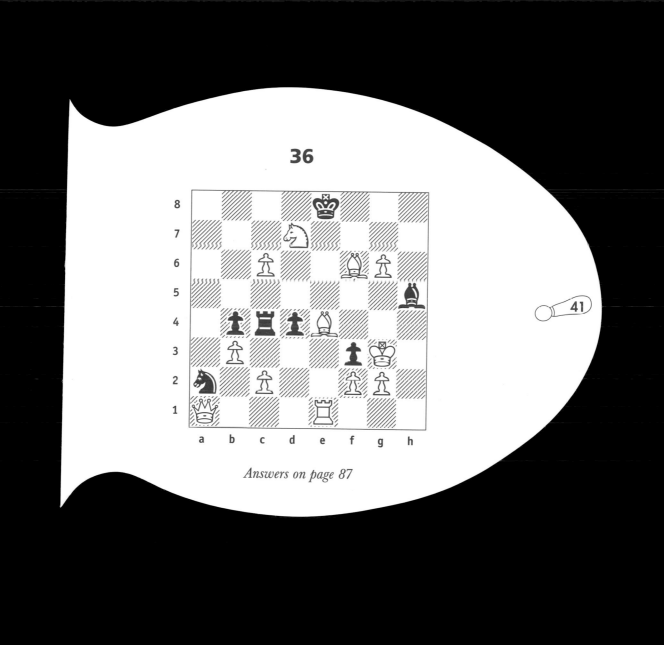

Answers on page 87

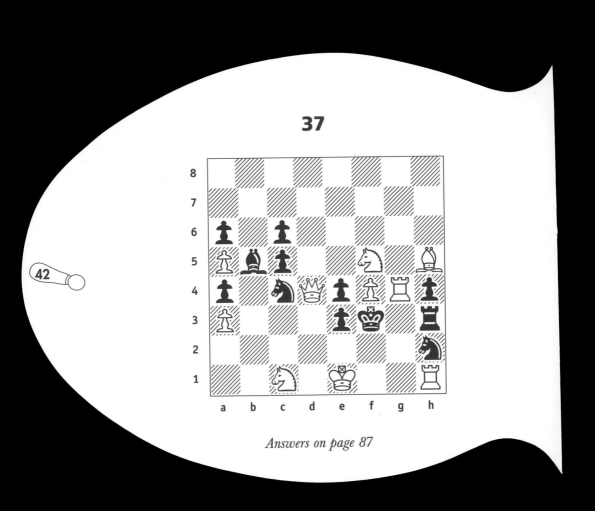

Answers on page 87

38

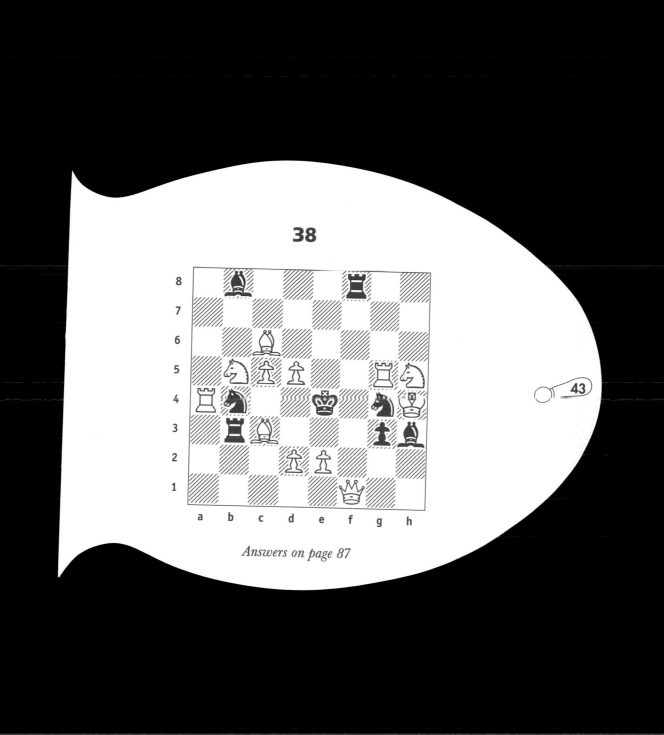

Answers on page 87

39

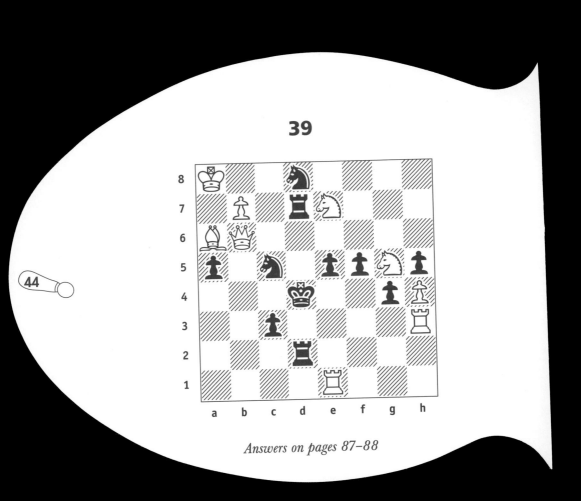

Answers on pages 87–88

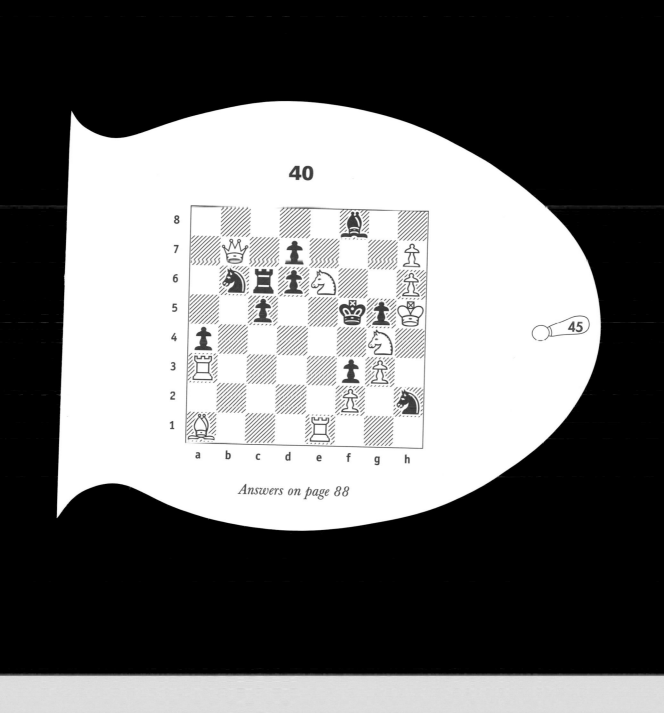

Answers on page 88

41

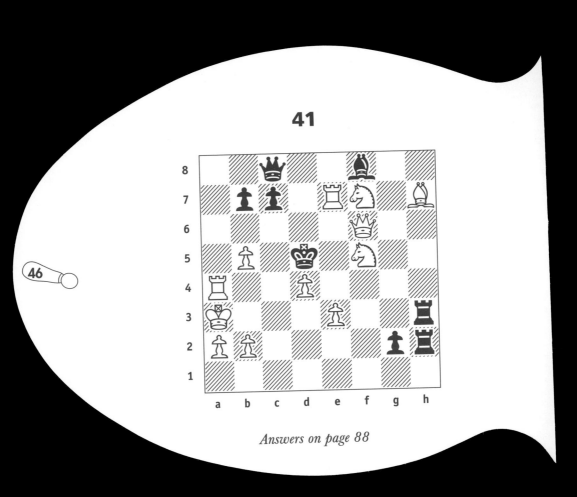

Answers on page 88

42

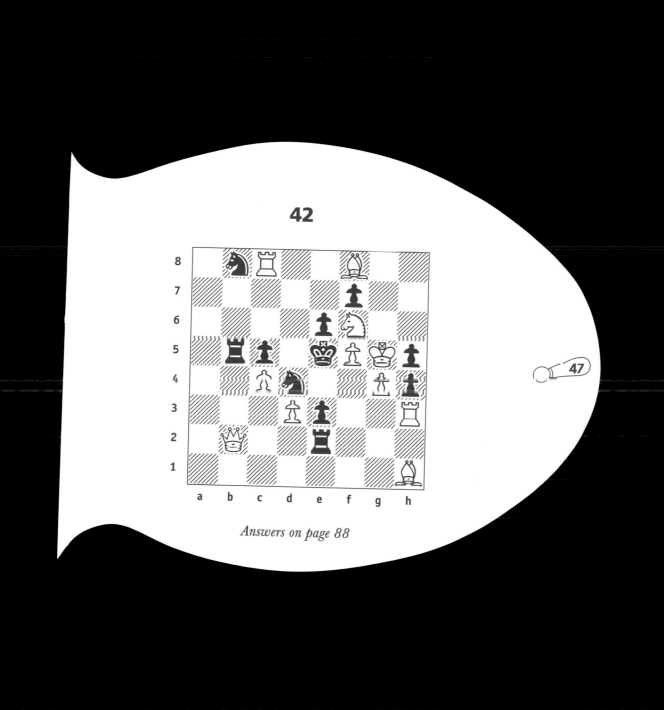

Answers on page 88

43

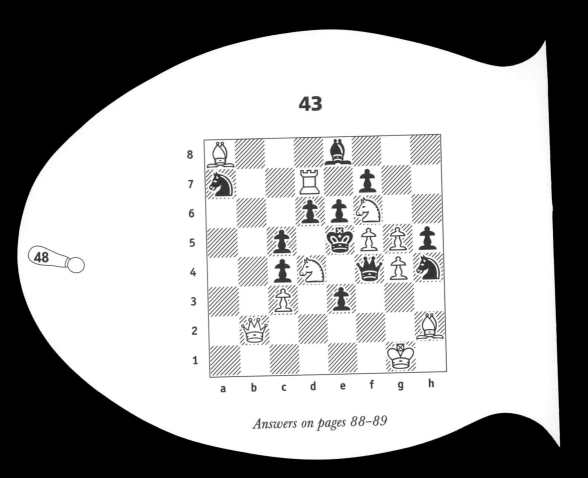

Answers on pages 88–89

48

44

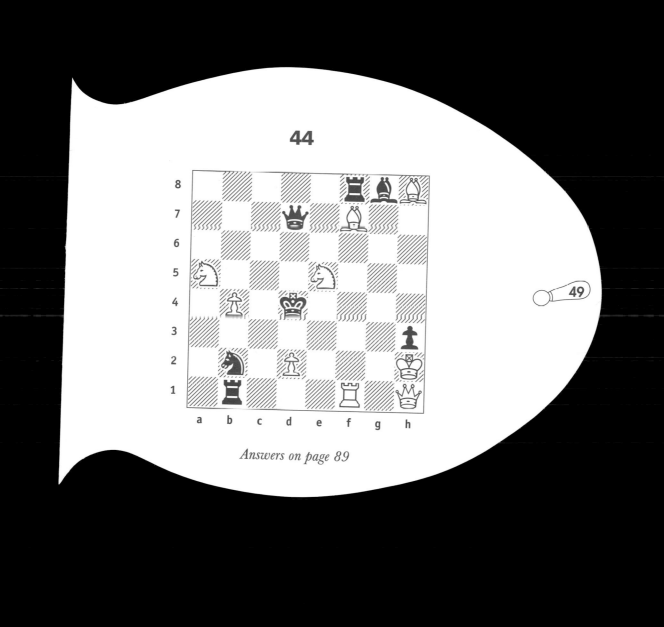

Answers on page 89

49

45

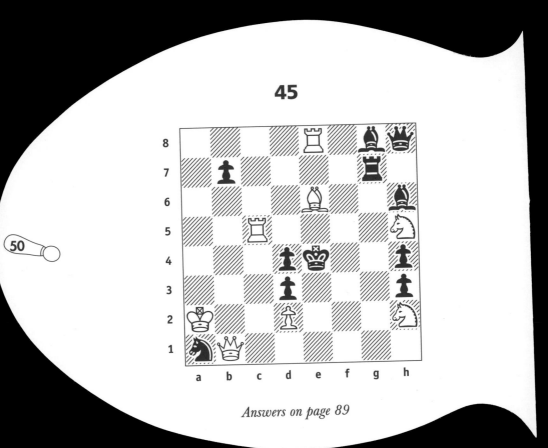

Answers on page 89

50

46

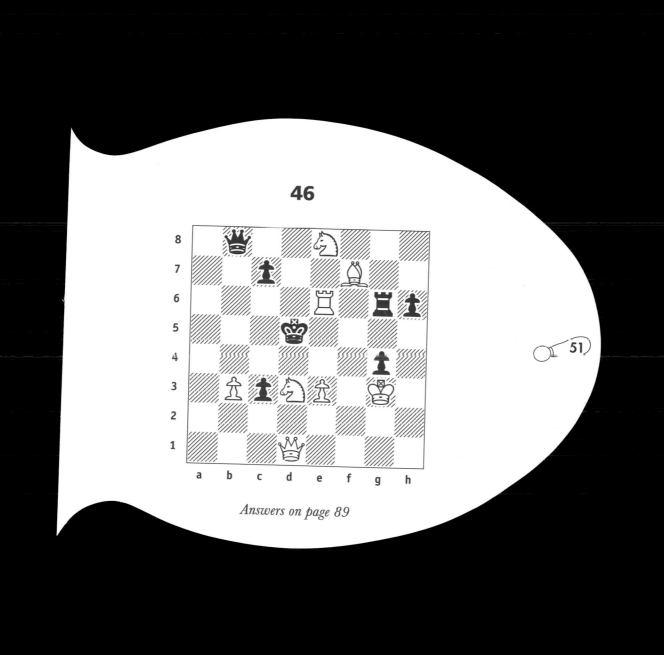

51

Answers on page 89

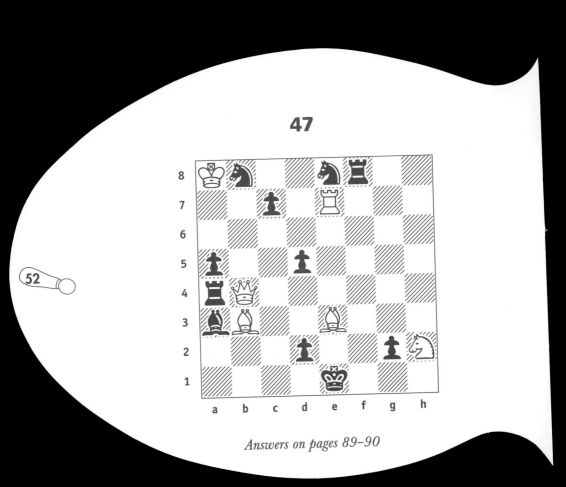

52

Answers on pages 89–90

48

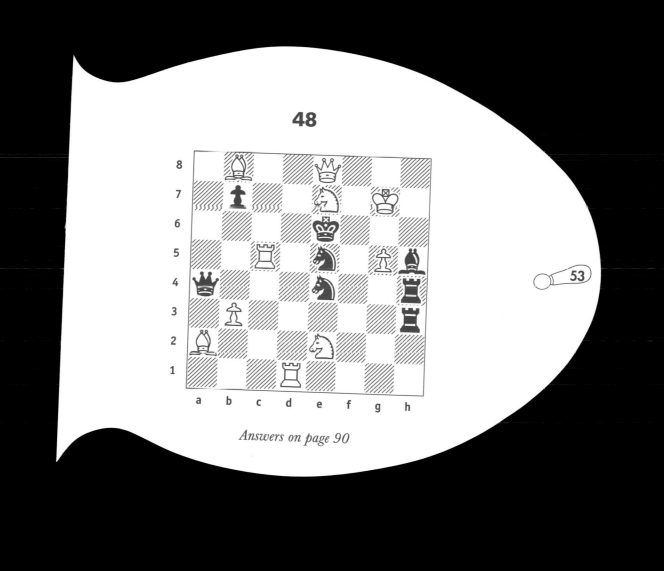

Answers on page 90

49

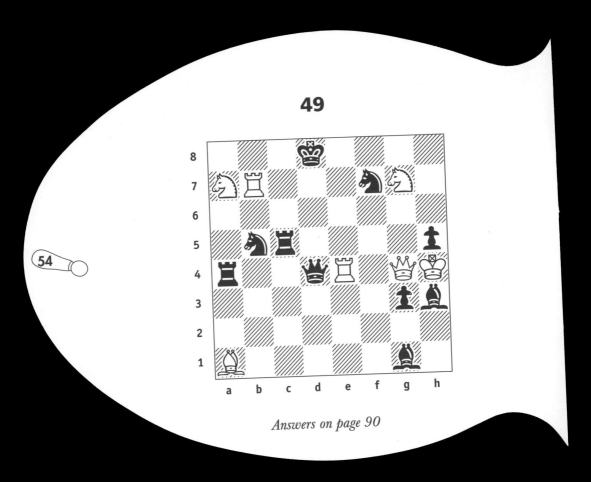

54

Answers on page 90

50

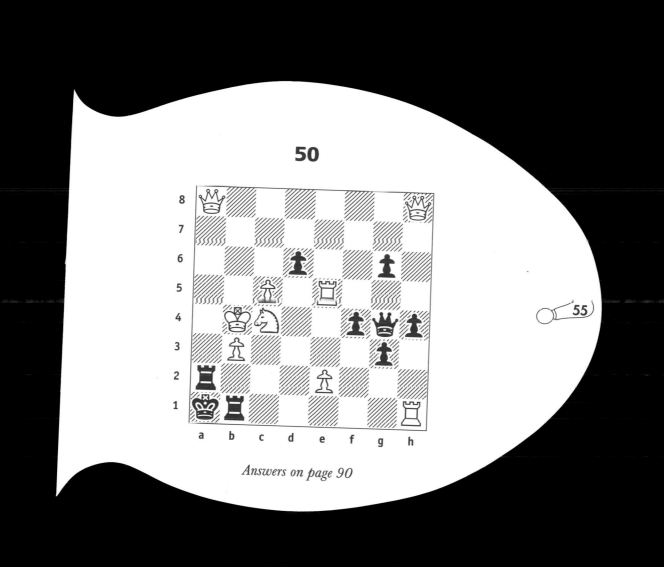

Answers on page 90

55

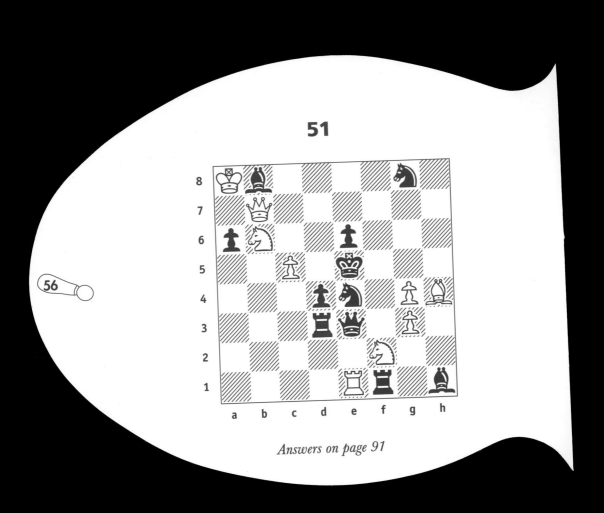

Answers on page 91

52

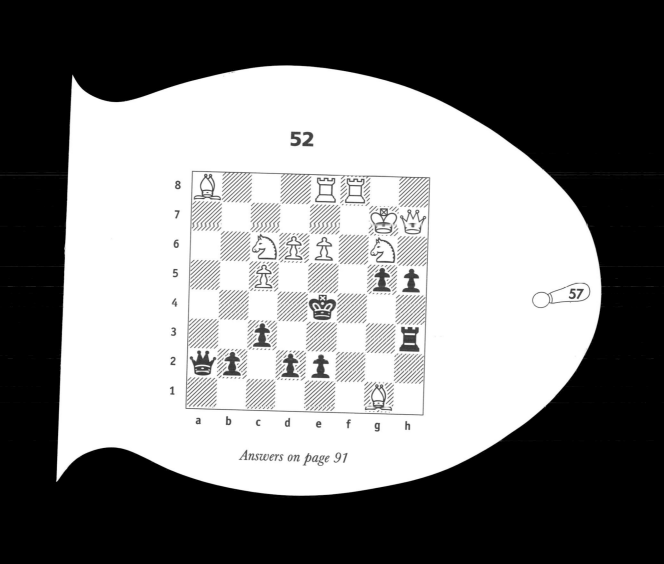

57

Answers on page 91

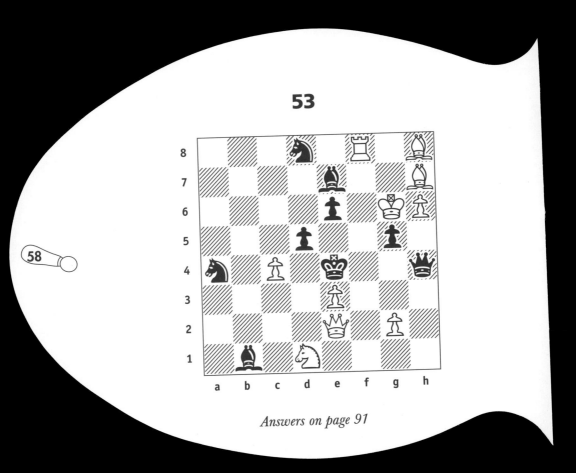

58

Answers on page 91

54

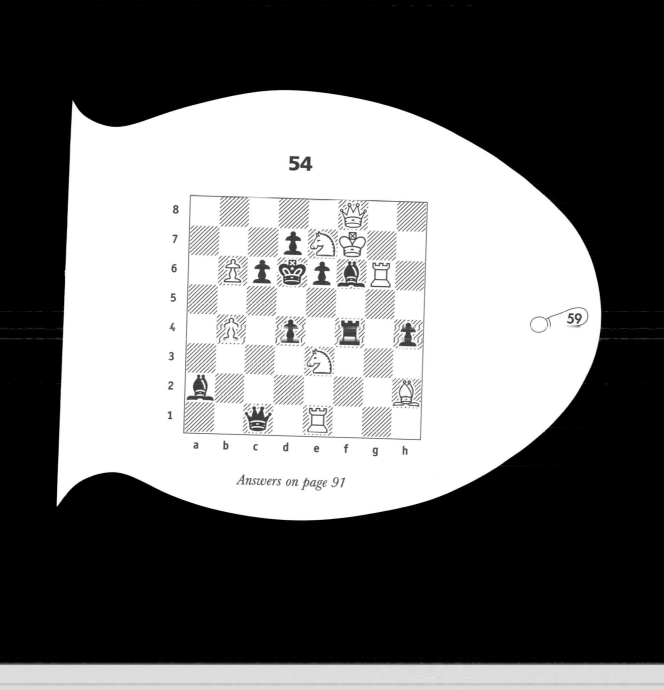

Answers on page 91

59

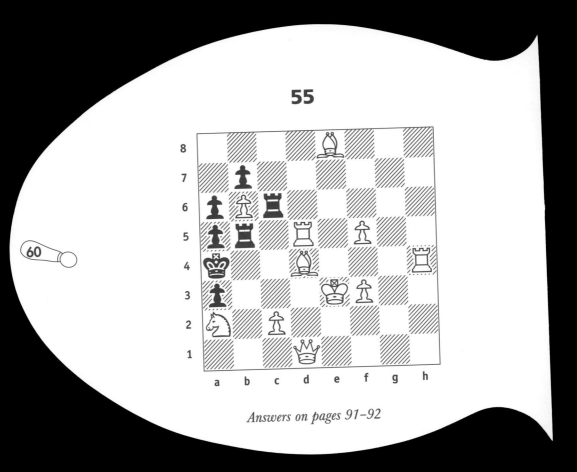

55

Answers on pages 91–92

60

56

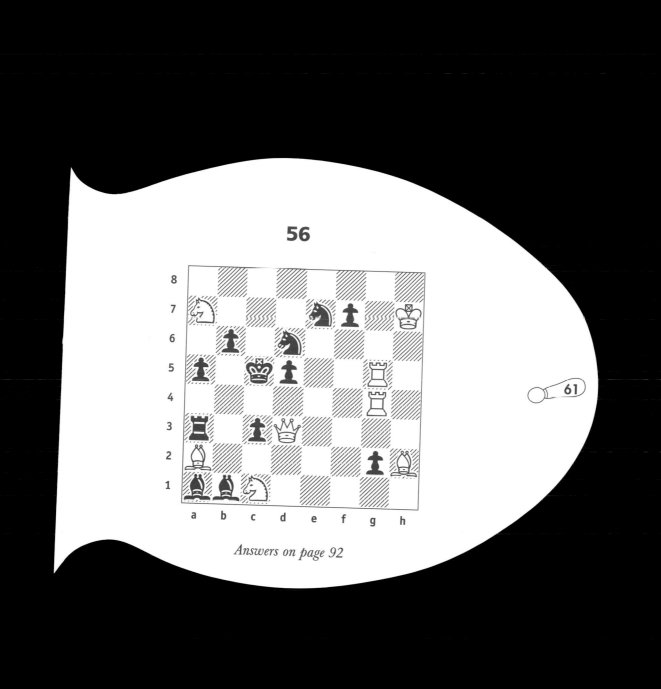

Answers on page 92

57

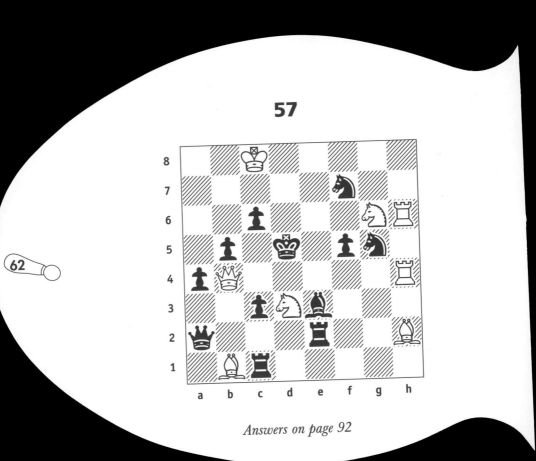

Answers on page 92

62

58

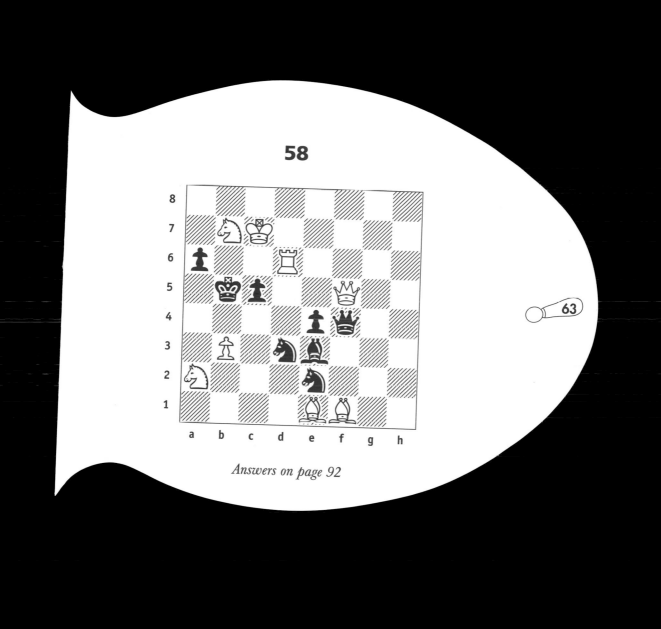

Answers on page 92

63

59

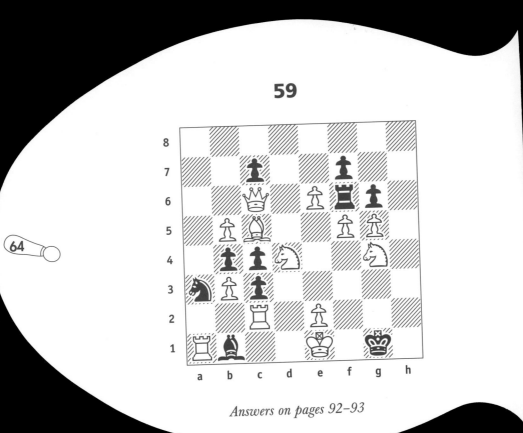

Answers on pages 92–93

60

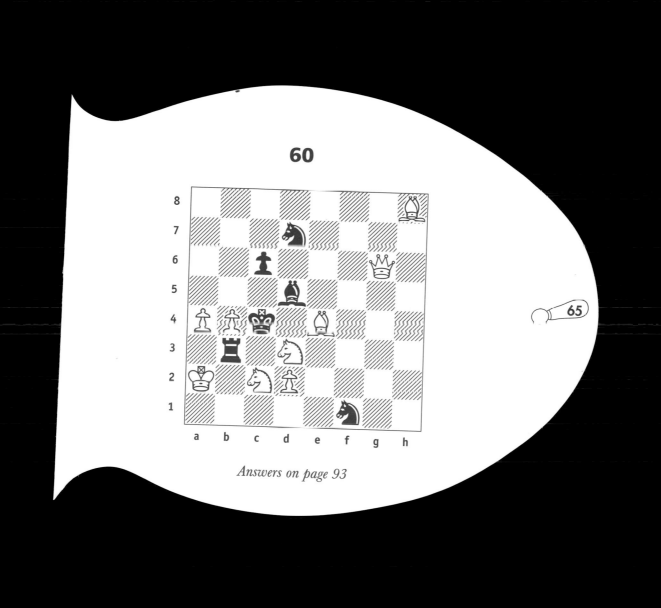

65

Answers on page 93

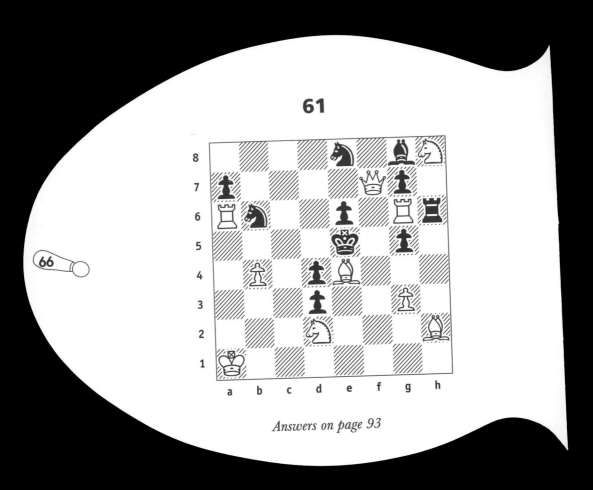

Answers on page 93

62

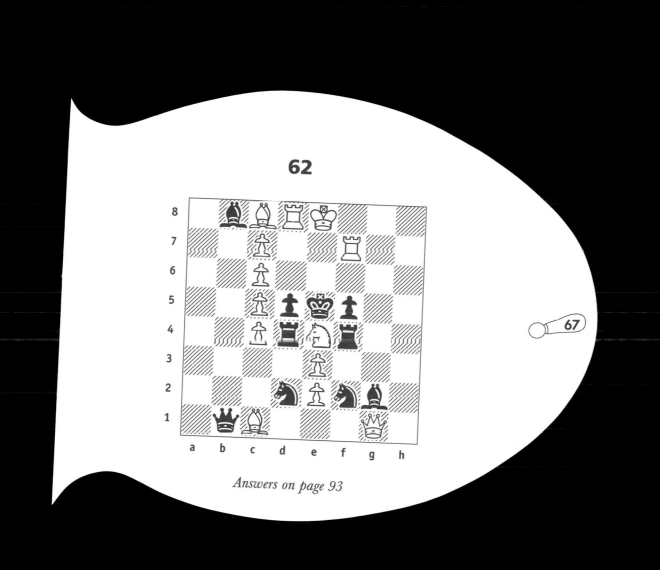

Answers on page 93

67

63

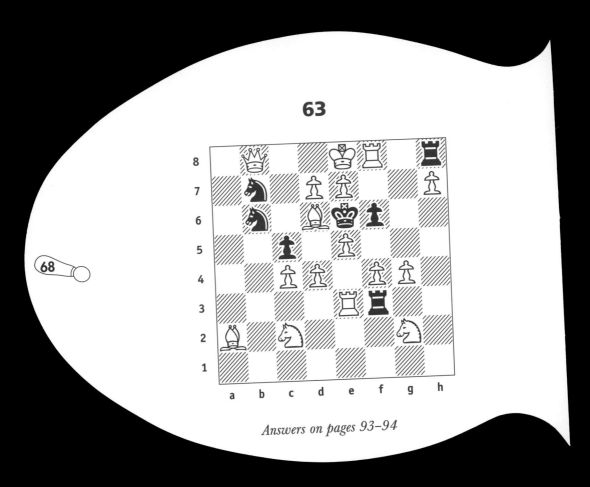

Answers on pages 93–94

68

64

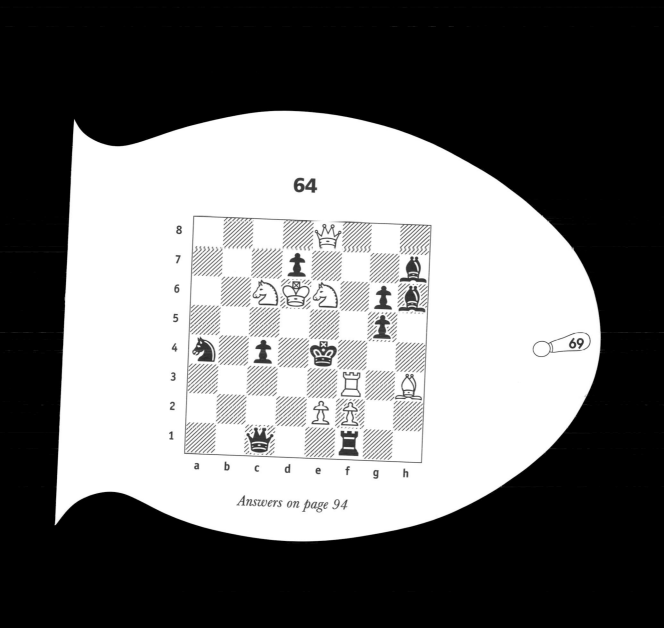

Answers on page 94

69

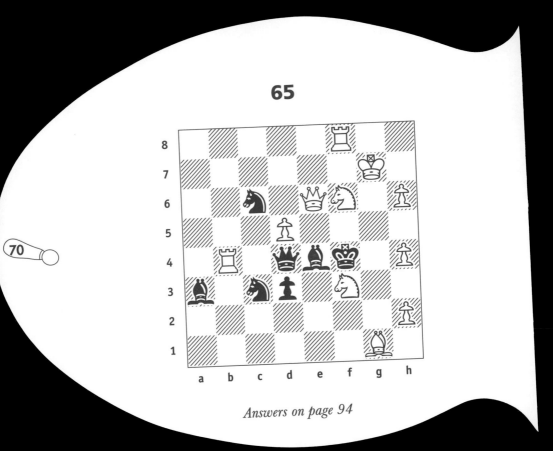

Answers on page 94

66

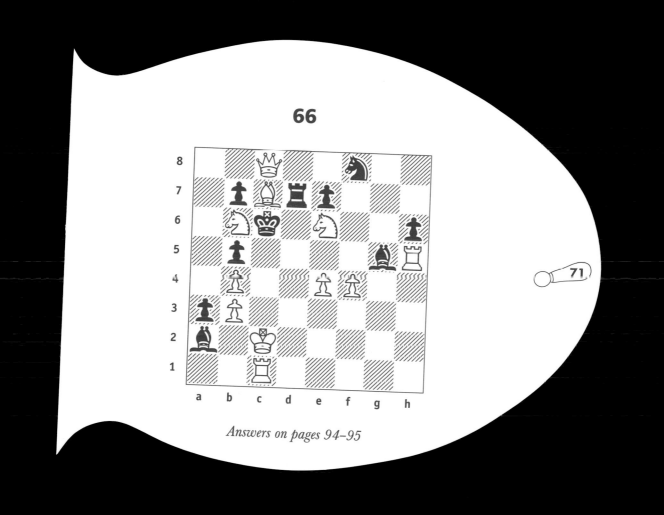

71

Answers on pages 94–95

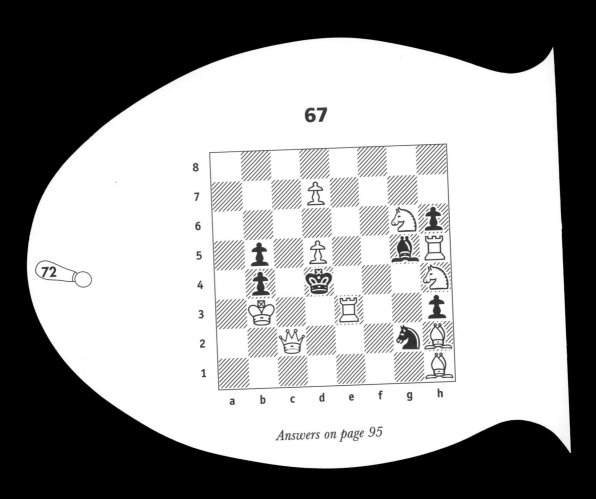

72

Answers on page 95

68

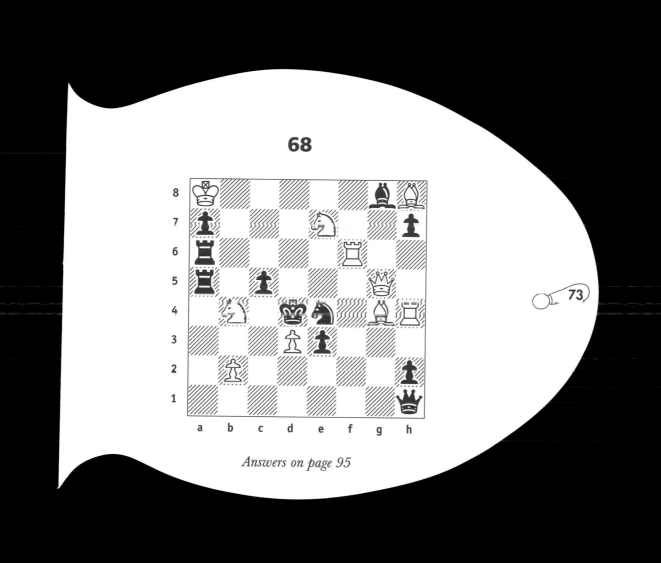

Answers on page 95

73

69

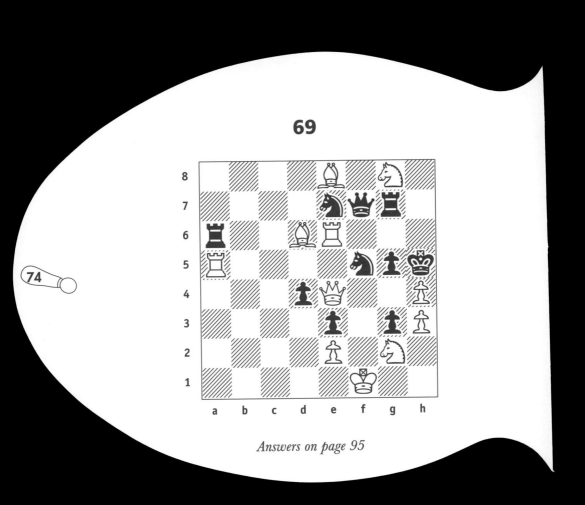

74

Answers on page 95

70

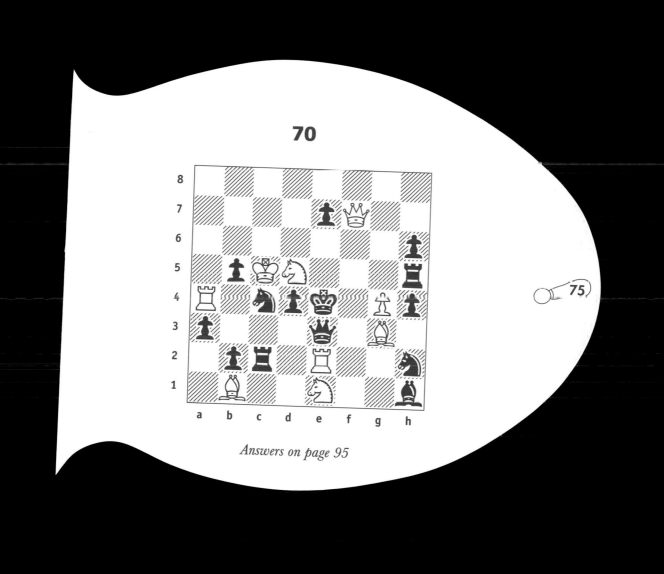

75

Answers on page 95

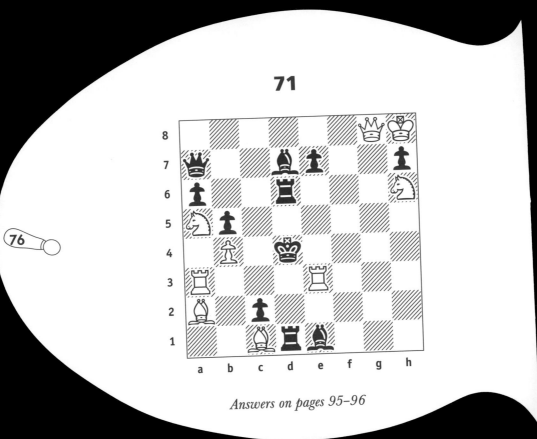

Answers on pages 95–96

72

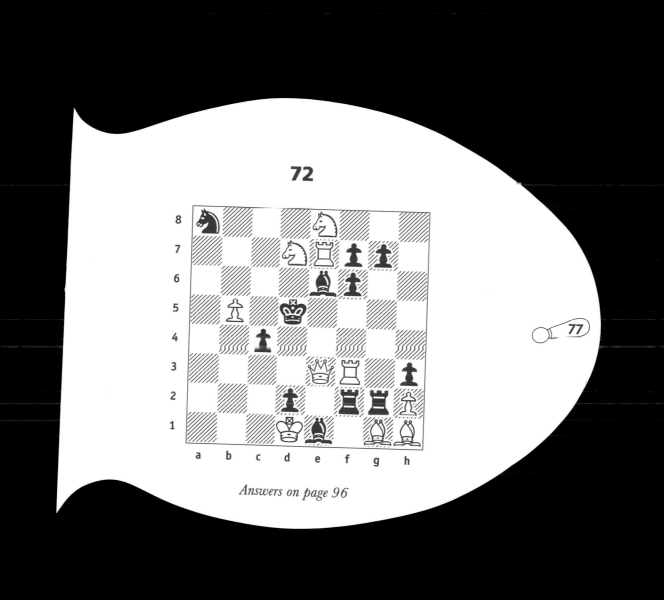

Answers on page 96

73

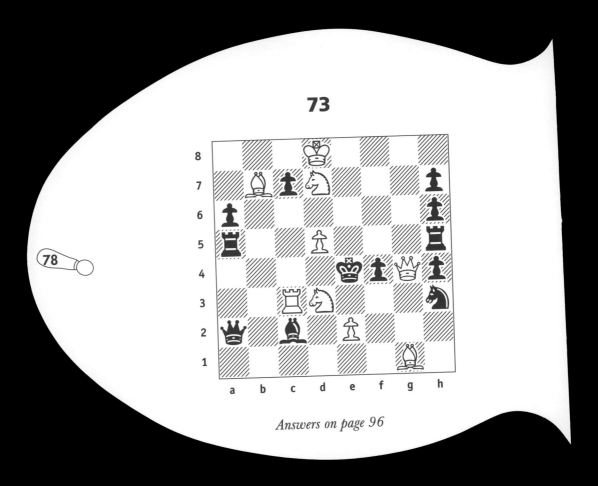

Answers on page 96

SOLUTIONS

Following the name of the composer and the source, there appears the word "Threat" or "Zugzwang." In a threat problem, White with his first move threatens to mate Black immediately with the specified move unless Black prevents it. Black can't, of course, but the various tries and White's answers to them demonstrate the composer's art. Zugzwang is a very important chess term that is particularly useful in the endgame. It means, literally, the compulsion, or necessity, to move when any move loses more or less directly. In a zugzwang problem, White does not threaten anything specific right away but sets the stage for the mate according to how Black plays.

The Black defenses in each solution given here are arranged according to the piece or pawn that is moving, in left-to-right order (files a–h, and from top to bottom (ranks 8–1). That is, defensive tries by pieces on the a-file come before those on the b-file, etc. For the sake of economy, moves by the same piece are bunched together but separated by a slash; thus 1 … Ne6/f7/g6/f5, etc. Moves by different pieces that are met by the same White mating move are separated by a comma: 1 … Rd7, Bd5 2 Qe6#. You may have to do a little searching for the move you want. The symbol ~ means "any"; thus 1 … B~ means any move by the bishop. Black defenses not found here are not relevant.

80

1 (from I. Aleshin, *Shakhmaty v SSSR*, 1946). Threat 2 Rb5#. 1 … Kxb4 2 Qc3#. 1 … Ncxb4 2 Nd7#. 1 ... Nd4 2 Rc4#. 1 … Ndxb4 2 Na4#. 1 ... Rxb4 2 Qc6#.

2 (from R. Amourette, *Miroir du Monde*, 1937). Threat 2 Qe6#, Nf4#. 1 … Bd5, Nd7 2 Nf4#. 1 … Nd5 2 Qe4#. 1 … Rd6 2 Qf5/g5/g7#, Nf4#. 1 … Rc6 2 Qf5/g5/e4/g7#,

Nf4#. 1 ... Rf6 2 Qg5#.
1 ... Rxe5+ 2 Nxc5#. 1 ... Rh7/h8 2 Qxe6#.
1 ... Rxh5 2 gxh5#.

3 (from I. Anderson, *Canadian Chess Chat*, 1981). Threat 2 Re5#.
1 ... Qa5/a1 2 Bc2#. 1 ... Bf6 2 Nxh6#. 1 ... Bc7 2 Ne7#. 1 ... Re6
2 Rf2#. 1 ... Rc5 2 Nd6#.

4 (from D. Andrieu, 1935). Threat 2 Nc3#. 1 ... Nc6 2 Qxc6#. 1 ... Kxe4+
2 Qc4#. 1 ... fxe4 2 Ne3#. 1 ... Rg3 2 Re5#. 1 ... Rxe2+ 2 Rxe2#.

5 (from T.M. Brown, *NY Albion*, 1960) Zugzwang. 1 ... c3 2 Qb4#.
1 ... dxe4 2 Rd2#. 1 ... d4 2 Qc6#. 1 ... fxe4 2 Rf6#. 1 ... f4 2 Qg6#.
1 ... Nd8/h8/h6/g5 2 Qxe5#.

6 (from A. Ianovcic, *Sachovy Svet*, 1925). Threat 2 Qxd6#. 1 ... Kc6+ 2 Nb6#.
1 ... Kd5+ 2 Nd4#. 1 ... Kb4+ 2 d4#.

7 (from A. Jakab, *Magyar Sakkelet 2*, 1925). Threat 2 Qh7#. 1 ... Ne5
2 Ncd4#. 1 ... Nf4 2 Ned4# 1 ... Rg2 2 e4#. 1 ... Bg7+ 2 Nxg7#.

8 (from F. Janet, *St. Louis Globe Democrat*, 1916). Threat
2 Qf5#. 1 ... Ra5 2 Qd4#. 1 ... Ne6 2 Nd5#.
1 ... e6 2 Qxa4#. 1 ... Nxe3 2 fxe3#.

1 ... Ng3 2 fxg3#. 1 ... Be6
2 Qxc7#.

9 (from F. Lazard, *L'Echiquier*, 1928). Zugzwang. 1 ... Bb6
2 Qxb6#. 1 ... Bc5 2 Qxc5#. 1 ... Bb8 2 Qb6/c5#. 1 ... Bb7/c8
2 c5#. 1 ... Bb5 2 cxb5#. 1 ... Bxc4 2 Qxc4#. 1 ... c2 2 Qb2#. 1 ... d2
2 Nc2#. 1 ... e5 2 Nf5#. 1 ... Nd8/h8/d6/h6/e5/g5 2 Q(x)d6#.

10 (from H. Prins, TM Belliboni, 1991) Threat 2 Ng3#. 1 ... Rd6 2 Nc3#.
1 ... Ndxe5 2 c4#. 1 ... fxe2/f2 2 Qh1#. 1 ... Ngxe5 2 f6#.

11 (from F.T. Vance, *Dubuque Chess Journal*, 1892). Threat 2 Qc6/d6/e6#.
1 ... c3 2 Qe6#. 1 ... d3 2 Qd6#. 1 ... e3 2 Qc6#.

12 (from White, 1906). Threat 2 Kd1#. 1 ... Nb2 2 Kxb2#. 1 ... Nc3
2 Kxc3#. 1 ... c3 2 Qd3#. 1 ... dxc1=Q+/R+/N+ 2 Kxc1#. 1 ... e5 2 Qd7#.
1 ... e2 2 Kxd2#. 1 ... Qf4 2 Rxf4#. 1 ... Qf3 2 Rxf3#. 1 ... Qxf1 2 Rxf1#.

13 (from White, 1918). Zugzwang. 1 ... Qxd7 2 Be4#. 1 ... Qd5 2 Bb5#.
1 ... Qd4 2 Rb3#. 1 ... e5 2 Qh3#. 1 ... B~ 2 Qh7#.

14 (from Yaroslavcev, date unk.). Threat 2 Nc3#. 1... Kb1
2 Nc3#. 1 ... bxa1=Q+/B+ 2 Nbd4#. 1 ... bxa1=R
2 Na5/c5/d4/d2/c1#. 1 ... bxa1=N

2 Nbc1#. 1 … b1=N 2 Nec1#.

15 (from B.P. Barnes, *The Problemist*, 2002).
Zugzwang. 1 … b6/b5 2 Kd6#. 1 … c3 2 Bxd5#. 1 … d4
2 Bxc4#. 1 … e4 2 Qxd5#. 1 … Nf8/xg5 2 R(x)f8#. 1 … Nxf6+
2 Qxf6#. 1 … gxh5 2 Qg7#.

16 (from A. Ellerman, Guidelli-Gedenk Turnier, 1925). Threat 2 Qf4#.
1 … Qd4 2 Nd6#. 1 … Qe5 2 Nc5#. 1 … Qf2 2 Nd8#. 1 … Bf2 2 Qxh1#.
1 … Bf3 2 Qd3#.

17 (from M. Lipton, *Il Due Mosse*, 1959). Zugzwang. 1 … Qxa2/c2
2 R(x)c2#. 1 … Qa1 2 Ne5, Rc2#. 1 … Qc1 2 Ne5#. 1 … Qxd3+
2 Qxd3#. 1 … Qd1 2 Ne5/xb2#. 1 … Qe1 2 Nxb2#. 1 … Qf1/g1/h1
2 Ne5/xb2, Rc2#. 1 … Ne8/g8/d7/h7/xd5/h5/g4 2 Qe4#. 1 … Ne4 2 Ne5, Qxe4#.

18 (from J. Hartong, *Probleemblad*, 1957). Zugzwang. 1 … Nxd7/xh7/e6, Kxg6
2 g8=Q#. 1 … Nfxg6, Nhxg6 2 Nd6#. 1 … Ke8 2 gxf8=Q/R#. 1 … Kc6
2 gxf8=N#. 1 … Kg8 2 gxh8=Q/R#.

19 (from M. Lipton, *The Problemist*, 1953). Threat 2 Rfxh3#.
1 … Qxf3+ 2 Bxf3#. 1 … Qg3 2 Rxg3#.
1 … Qg2/f1/xg4 2 R(x)f1#.

1 ... Qxh7+ 2 Rf5#.
1 ... Qh6 2 Rf6/f1#. 1 ... Qh5 2 Rf5/f1#.
1 ... Bg3 2 Rf2#.

20 (from M. R. Vukcevic, *Die Schwalbe*, 1961). Threat 2 c3/c4#.
1 ... b3 2 cxb3#. 1 ... Nxd3 2 cxd3#. 1 ... Bxe5 2 c3#. 1 ... Ne3
2 Qxe3#. 1 ... Bg8 2 c4#.

21 (from J. Hartong, *Jaarboek N.B. v P.*, 1952). Zugzwang. 1 ... Bd7, Rd5,
Bd6 2 Q(x)d5#. 1 ... Be6, Re5, Be7 2 Q(x)e5#. 1 ... Bf5/b7, Rd7, Re6
2 N(x)f5#. 1 ... Rd6 2 Qxb4#. 1 ... Re7, Bg7, Bh6 2 Qxb4/b6#.
1 ... Bc5 2 Qa1#.

22 (from K.A.K. Larsen, *Good Companion*, 1919). Threat 2 Qe6#.
1 ... Bd6 2 Bc6#. 1 ... Be5 2 Qxh1#. 1 ... Nc5 2 Nc3#. 1 ... Nd4 2 Bc4#.
1 ... Be4 2 Qxe4#.

23 (from Oey Gian Tiong, *Problem*, 1967). Threat 2 Nc3#. 1 ... N6xd4
2 a8=Q/B#. 1 ... N2xd4 2 Bxc6#.1 ... Bxd4 2 Nf6#. 1 ... Ke4 2 Nc3#.
1 ... Rxd4 2 Qg2#.

24 (from D.J. Shire, *The Problemist Suppl.*, 1997).
Zugzwang. 1 ... Bb1/b3 2 Q(x)b3#.

1 ... Nxa4 2 Qxa4#. 1 ... Nd1
2 Qxa2#. 1 ... Rd5/d6/d7/d8/d1 2 Qxc3#.
1 ... Rd4 2 Ne5#. 1 ... Re3/d2+ 2 N(x)d2#. 1 ... Rxf3
2 Qe4#.

25 (from C.F. Stubbs, *St. John's Globe*, 1891). Zugzwang. 1 ... c3
2 Qxc3#. 1 ... d2 2 Rxd2#. 1 ... e5 2 Qxa7#. 1 ... Nd8/ h8/d6/h6/g5
2 Q(x)d6#. 1 ... Ne5 2 Qxa7/d6#. 1 ... g3 2 Rh4#.

26 (from J.M. Rice, 1915). Threat 2 Qe7#. 1 ... b5 2 Qa5#. 1 ... c5 2 Nb5#.
1 ... Rc5 2 Rh7#. 1 ... Rd5 2 Rxc6#. 1 ... Re5, Bd6 2 Q(x)d6#.

27 (from G. Jönsson, *Schachvärlden*, 1939). Zugzwang. 1 ... Nb6 2 Rxb6#.
1 ... Nb4 2 Rxb4#. 1 ... Nc7 2 Rxc7#. 1 ... Nxa3 2 Rb3#. 1 ... Ne7
2 Rxe7#. 1 ... Ne3 2 Rf2#. 1 ... Nxf6 2 Rf7#. 1 ... Nf4 2 Nd4#.

28 (from F. Istokovics, *L'Echiquier Belge*, 1981-82). Threat 2 Qxe3#. 1 ... Nc4
2 Nb5#. 1 ... Re7 2 Qxd5#. 1 ... exd2 2 Qxd3#. 1 ... Bxf1 2 Qxf4#.
1 ... Bf2 2 Ne6#.

29 (from X. Hawkins, *La Presse*, 1898). Zugzwang. 1 ... Nb3/
d3/e2 2 N(x)d3#. 1 ... d3 2 Qe5#. 1 ... dxe3 2
Qa4#. 1 ... f2 2 Qb8#. 1 ... fxg2

2 N1xg2#. 1 ... Bxg6
2 Rxf3#. 1 ... Bg4 2 Nd5#.

30 (from K. Arnstam, *Raketa,* 1941). Threat 2 Qxd6#.
1 ... Kd5 2 Qxd6#. 1 ... Nc8/e8/xc4 2 Qxd4#, Qxd4#. 1 ...
N6b5 2 Qxb4#. 1 ... N6f5 2 Nd3#. 1 ... Ne4 2 Qxd4/Nd3/Qxd4#.
1 ... N4b5 2 Qxb6#. 1 ... N4f5 2 Nd7#. 1 ... Bd7 2 Qxd4#.

31 (from F. Andrade, *Boletim de UBP,* 1962). Threat 2 Nxc6, Nxf5#. 1 ... Nc7+
2 dxc7#. 1 ... Qg4/xf4/h5/xh3/g5/f6 2 Nxc6#. 1 ... Nxe5 2 Nb3#. 1 ... Nd2/xe1
2 Ne2#. 1 ... Qxe7+ 2 dxe7#. 1 ... Qxf2 2 Nxf5#.

32 (from G.C. Alvey, *The Observer,* 1920). Threat 2 Rc5#. 1 ... Nd5, Rd5
2 Nc6#. 1 ... Rd4 2 e8=Q/R#. 1 ... Kd4 2 Rc6/xc7#. 1 ... Bd5+
2 Rc4#. 1 ... Bc6/b7/xa8/xf5 2 Rcxd3#. 1 ... Bd4 2 Nd3#.

33 (from F. Janet, *St. Louis Globe Democrat,* 1916). Threat 2 Qf5#. 1 ... Ra5
2 Qd4#. 1 ... Ne6 2 Nd5#. 1 ... e6 2 Qxa4#. 1 ... Nxe3 2 fxe3#. 1 ... Be6
2 Qxc7#. 1 ... Ng3 2 fxg3#.

34 (from D. Andrieu, *Miroir du Monde,* 1937). Threat 2 Rc5#.
1 ... Rc6, Bxc4 2 Nd7#. 1 ... Bc6 2 Bxd6#. 1 ... Be3
2 Nf3#. 1 ... Rxd4 2 Qxd4#. 1 ... Re3, Nf4,

Ba3 2 Rxg5#. 1 ... Ne3 2 Qg3#.

35 (from R. Aumont, *Casssa*, 1943). Threat 3
Qd5#. 1 ... Nb6/d6/a3/b2/d2 2 Re1#. 1 ... Ne3 2 Nd2#. 1
... Rxf3+ 2 gxf3#. 1 ... Bxc5 2 Nxc5#.

36 (from G. Authier, *Le Problème*, 1949). Threat 2 Bxf3, Bd3#. 1 ...
Nc3/c1 1 Qa8#. 1.., Bg4 2 Bf5# 1 ... Rxc6 2 Bxc6#. 1 ... Rc5 2 Bd5#.
1 ... Rc3 2 Bd3#. 1 ... Rxc2 2 Bxc2#. 1 ... d3 2 Qe5#. 1 ... fxg2 2 Bf3#.
1 ... Bxg6 2 Bxg6#.

37 (from F. Daniel, *Szachi*, 1959). Zugzwang. 1 ... cxd4 2 Nxd4#
1 ... Nb6/d6/xa5/e5/xa3/b2/d2 2 Qxe3#. 1 ... e2 2 Qf2#. 1 ... Rg3
2 Nxh4#. 1 ... Nxg4 2 0-0#. 1 ... Nf1 Rxf1#.

38 (from S. Ekstrom and G. Andersson, *Tidskrift for Schack*, 1947). Threat 2 d6#.
1 ... Bd6 2 Nxd6# 1 ... Rc8 2 Qxf3/f5#. 1 ... Rf5 2 Qxf5#. 1 ... Nf6 2 Qf3#.
1 ... Ne5 2 Nxg3#. 1 ... Ne3 2 d3#.

39 (from W. Grimshaw, *Ill. London News XI*, 1870). Zugzwang.
1 ... a4 2 Qb4#. 1 ... c2 2 Qb2#. 1 ... Ndxb7/f7/c6/e6
2 N(x)e6#. 1 ... Rc7/xb7/xe7/d6 2 Q(x)d6#.
1 ... Rd5 2 Nxf5#.

1 ... Rc2/b2/a2/d3/e2/f2/
g2/h2 2 R(x)d3#. 1 ... Rd1 2 Rxd1#.
1 ... e4 2 Qf6#. 1 ... f4 2 Re4#. 1 ... gxh3/g3 2 Nf3#.

40 (from J. Hartong, *Tijdschrift*, 1918). Zugzwang. 1 ...
Na8/c8/d5/c4 2 Qb1#. 1 ... Rc7/c8 2 Qe4#. 1 ... c4 2 Nd4#. 1 .. dxe6
2 Qf7#. 1 ... d5 2 Re5#. 1 ... Bg7/e7 2 N(x)g7#. 1 ... Bxh6 2 Nxh6#.
1 ... Nxg4/f1 2 Rxf3#.

41 (from F. Istokovics, Jubilé Szoghi-70, 1981) Threat 2 Qe5#). 1 ... Qe6
2 Qxe6#. 1 ... Qxf5 2 Qxf5#. 1 ... Bg7 2 Re5#. 1 ... Bxe7+ 2 Nxe7#.
1 ... Rxe3+ 2 Nxe3#.

88

42 (from T. Kardos and Takacs, *Magyar Sakkvilag*, 1949). Zugzwang.
1 ... Nd7/a6/c6 2 N(x)d7#. 1 ... Ra5 2 Qxb8#. 1 ... Rb6/b7/b4/b3/xb2
2 Rxc5#. 1 ... exf5 2 Rxc5#. 1 ... Rh2 2 Rxe3, Qxh2#. 1 ... Re1 2 Qh2#.
1 ... Rd2/c2/xb2/f2/g2 2 Rxe3#. 1 ... hxg4 2 Nxg4#.

43 (from A. Karlstrom, *The Chess Problem*, 1947). Zugzwang.
1 ... Nc8/c6/b5 2 N(x)c6#. 1 ... cxd4 2 cxd4#. 1 ... d5 2 Qb8#.
1 ... Bxd7 2 Nxd7#. 1 ... e2 2 Qxe2#. 1 ... exf5 2 Re7#.
1 ... Qg3+ 2 Bxg3#. 1 ... Qxh2+ 2 Qxh2#.

1 ... hxg4 2 Nxg43. 1 ... Ng6/
xf5/f3+/g2 2 N(x)f3#.

44 (from A. Kempe, *Chess Player's Chronicle*, 1853). Threat
2 Nb3, Rf4#. 1 ... Nd3 2 Nec6#. 1 ... Qa4 2 Rf4, Qd5#. 1 ... Qc6
2 Naxc6/b3#. 1 ... Qd5 2 Qxd5#. 1 ... Qxf7 2 Nac6#. 1 ... Qf5/g4
2 Nac6/b3, Qd5#. 1 ... Rxf7, Bh7, Qb7, Re1/xf1 2 Nb3#. 1 ... Bxf7, Qe6,
Na4/c4/d1 2 Rf4#.

45 (from L. Kubbel, *Tijdskrift for Schack*, 1917). Threat 2 Bf7#. 1 ... Bxe6+ 2
Rxe6#. 1 ... Bf7, Rg6/g4/g3/g2/g1 2 Qxb7#. 1 ... Bh7, Rf7 2 Bf5#.
1 ... Re7/d7/c7/h7, Bg5 2 Qh1#. 1 ... Rg5 2 Qe1#. 1 ... Bf4 2 Nf5#.

46 (from L. Kubbel, *Sydney Herald*, 1908). Threat 2 Qh1#. 1 ... Qb4 2
Nxc7#. 1 ... Qxb3 2 Qxb3#. 1 ... c6+ 2 Re5#. 1 ... c5+ 2 Nf4#. 1 ... Rf6 2
Nxf6#.

47 (from L. Kubbel, *Kagan Sakk-konyvkiai*, 1922). Threat 2 Qxd2, Bg1, Bd4,
Bc5, Bb6, Ba7#. 1 ... axb4+ 2 Ba7#. 1 ... Rxb4 2 Bd4#. 1 ... Bxb4 2
Bc5#. 1 ... Bb2 2 Qxd2, Bd4#. 1 ... Bc1 2 Bg1/d4/c5/b6/a7#. 1
... Nd7/c6, Ng7/d6/f6, Rf7/f6/f5/f4/f3, Ke3 2 Qxd2#.
1 ... c5 2 Qxd2, Bg1/d4/xc5#. 1 ... d4 2

Qxd2, Bg1/xd4#. 1 … Rf2
2 Bxd2# 1 … g1=Q/B/N 2 Qxd2, Bxg1#.

48 (from A. Mari, Il Sekolo Tournoi 1921). Threat 2
Rxe5#. 1 … Nd7 2 Ng6#. 1 … Nf7 2 Nc6#. 1 … Nc6 2 Qd7#.
1 … Ng6 2 Qf7#. 1 … Nc4, Qa5/d4/b5 2 N(x)d4#. 1 … Ng4 2 Nf4#.
1 … Nd3/f3 2 bxa4#. 1 … Nd6/xc5 2 R(x)d6#.

49 (from Marshall, 1941). Threat 2 Re8#. 1 … Nc7 2 Rb8#. 1 … Nfd6, Nbd6,
Qd7/xe4/e5/xg7 2 R(x)d7#. 1 … Re5 2 Nc6#. 1 … Ne5 2 Qg5#. 1 … Qe3
2 Rd7, Bf6#. 1 … Qf6+ 2 Bxf6#.

90   **50** (from N. Petrovic, *Sahovski Vjesnik*, 1948). Threat 2 Rd5, Re6, Re7,
Re8, Rf5, Rg5, Rh5, Re4, Re3#. 1 … dxc5 2 Rxc5#. 1 … d5 2 Rxd5#.
1 … dxe5 2 Qxe5#. 1 … f3 2 Re4#. 1 … g5 2 Rd5/e6/e7/e8/f5/xg5/e4/e3#.
1 … Qc8 2 Re8#. 1 … Qd7 2 Re7#. 1 … Qe6 2 Rxe6#. 1 … Qxe2 2 Rxe2#.
1 … Qf5 2 Rxf5#. 1 … Qf3 2 Re3#. 1 … Qg5 2 Rxg5#. 1 … Qh5 2 Rxh5#.
1 … Rxa8 2 Qxa8#. 1 … Ra7 2 Qxa7#. 1 … Ra6 2 Qxa6#. 1 … Ra5
2 Qxa5#. 1 … Ra4+ 2 Qxa4#. 1 … Ra3 2 Qxa3#. 1 … Rc1
2 Rxc1#. 1 … Rd1 2 Rxd1#. 1 … Re1 2 Rxe1#. 1… Rf1
2 Rxf1#. 1 … Rg1 2 Rxg1#. 1 … Rxh1 2 Qxh1#.

51 (from A. Pituk, *Magyar Sakkelet* 7, 1955). Threat 2 Nd7, Nc4#. 1 … Nd6/d2 2 Nd7, Nxd3#. 1 … Nef6 2 Nc4, Nxd3#. 1 … Ng5, Rc3, Qg5 2 Nd7#. 1 … Nxg3 2 Nxd3#. 1 … Ngf6, Nxc5 2 Nc4#. 1 … Qc1 2 Qxb8, Nd7, Nxd3#. 1 … Qxg3 2 Qxb8#.

52 (from I.A. Schiffmann, *Observer*, 1928). Threat 2 Nge7#. 1 … Qxe6 2 Nb4#. 1 … Kd5 2 Na5#. 1 … Kd3, Qd5 2 Nge5#. 1 … Rf3 2 Nf4#.

53 (from G.J. Slater, *Leeds Mercury*, 1897) Zugzwang. 1 … Nb6/c5/c3/b2 2 N(x)c3#. 1 … Ba2/c2 2 Q(x)c2#. 1 … Nb7/f7/c6/ 2 K(x)f7#. 1 … dxc4 2 Qxc4#. 1 … d4 2 exd4#. 1 … Bf6/d6/c5/b4/a3/xf8 2 K(x)f6#. 1 … e5 2 Kg7# 1 … Qf4 2 cxf4#. 1 … g4 2 Rf4#. 1 … Qg4/h3/h2/h1/f2 2 N(x)f2#. 1 … Qxh6+ 2 Kxh6#. 1 … Qh5+/g3/e1 2 K(x)h5#. 1 … Bd3 2 Qf3#.

54 (from G. Guidelli, *L'Eco degli Scacchi*, 1916). Threat 2 Qb8#. 1 … Ke5 2 Nc4#. 1 … e5+ 2 N7d5#. 1 … Bxe7+ 2 Bxf4#. 1 … Be5+ 2 N7f5#. 1 … Bg5+/g7+/h8+ 2 N3f5#.

55 (from J.M. Rice, *The Observer*, 1963). Zugzwang. 1 … Rbxb6 2 Bxb6#. 1 … Rbc5/xd5 2 c4#. 1 … Rb4 2 Nc3#. 1 … Rb3+ 2 cxb3#. 1 … Rb2/b1 2

B(x)b2#. 1 ... Rcxb6 2
Bc3/b2/ a1/c5/xb6/e5/f6/g7/h8#, c3/c4#.
1 ... Rc7/c8/c5 2 Bc5#, c3/c4#. 1 ... Rc4 2 c3#.
1 ... Rc3+ 2 Bxc3#. 1 ... Rxc2 2 Qxc2#. 1 ... Rd6
2 Bc3/b2/a1/c5/e5/f6/g7/h8#, c3/c4#. 1 ... Re6+ 2 Be5#. 1 ... Rf6
2 Bc3/b2/a1/c5/e5/xf6#, c3/c4#. 1 ... Rg6/h6 2 c3/c4#.

56 (from V. Bernstein and G. Gaidarov, Issaev Mem., 1933). Threat 2 Bg1#.
1 ... Ra4/x2 2 Nb3#. 1 ... Bxd3+ 2 Nxd3#. 1 ... c2 2 Qxa3#. 1 ... Nef5
2 Qxd5#. 1 ... Ne4 2 Qc4#. 1 ... Ndc8/e8/b7/b5/c4 2 R(x)c4#.
1 ... Nc6 2 Rxd5#. 1 ...Ndf5 2 Qb5#. 1 ... f5 2 Qd4#.

57 (from N.A. Macleod, *Christian Science Monitor*, 1948). Threat 2 Ne7#.
1 ... Ke6, Bc5 2 Ngf4#. 1 ... Bd4 2 Ndf4#. 1 ... Bd2 2 Bxa2#. 1 ... Bf2/g1/b6/
a7/f4 2 Ngf4, Ndf4#. 1 ... Nd6+/xh6 2 Q(x)d6#.

58 (from A. Baron, *Bulletin de la FFE*, 1938), Threat 2 Qd7#. 1 ... Nb4
2 Nc3#. 1 ... Nd4 2 Qxc5#. 1 ... Qxd6+ 2 Nxd6#. 1 ... Qxf5/g4, Ne5
2 Rb6#.

59 (from B. Gruber). Zugzwang. 1 ... Nxb5 2 Nxb5#.
1 ... Nxc2+, Bxc2 2 Nxc2#. 1 ... Ba2 2 0-0-0#.

1 … cxb3 2 Nxb3#. 1 … fxe6,
Rxe6 2 Nxe6#. 1 … Rxf5, gxf5 2 Nxf5#.

60 (from J. Hartong, *Western Morning News and Mercury*,
1919). Zugzwang. 1 … Ra3+/xb4/b1 2 N(x)a3#. 1 … Rc3/b2+
2 N(x)b2#. 1… Rxd3 2 Bxd3#. 1 … c5 2 Qa6#. 1 … Nb8/f8/b6/f6/c5/e5
2 N(x)e5#. 1 … Bxe4 2 Qxe4#. 1 … Be6 2 Qxe6#. 1 … Bf7 2 Qxf7#.
1 … Bg8 2 Qxg8#. 1 … Ne3/g3/xd2/h2 2 N(x)e3#.

61 (from N.A. Izvolskij, *Shakhmaty Jurnal,* 1892). Zugzwang. 1 … Nb 2~ 2
Raxe6, Rxg5#. 1 … Nc7/f6 2 Q(x)c7#. 1 … Nd6 2 Qxg7#. 1 … Kd6
2 Nc4#. 1 … Bxf7 2 Nxf7#. 1 … Bh7 2 Qxe6#. 1 … g4 2 Qf4#.
1 … Rxg6 2 g4#. 1 … Rh7/xh8/h5/h3/xh2 2 Rxe6#. 1 … Rh4
2 Rxe6, gxh4#.

62 (from G. Neukomm, *Deutsches Wochenschach,* 1916). Threat 2 Re7#. 1 … Bxe4
2 Qg7#. 1 … Qxe4 2 cxb8=Q/B#. 1 … dxe4, Nfxe4 2 exd4#. 1 … Rdxe4
2 Rxd5#. 1 … Kxe4 2 Re7#. 1 … fxe4, Ndxe4 2 exf4#. 1 … Rfxe4 2 Rxf5#.

63 (from N. Petrovic, 1947). Zugzwang. 1 … Na5 2 d8=N#. 1 …
Nd8 2 exd8=N#. 1 … Nxd6+ 2 Qxd6#. 1 … Na8/xd7/
a4 2 d5#. 1 … Nc8 2 dxc8=Q/B, d5#.

1 … Nxc4 2 Bxc4#.

1 … Nd5 2 cxd5#. 1 … cxd4 2 Nxd4#.

1 … fxe5 2 Rxe5#. 1 … f5 2 gxf5#. 1 … Rxf8+

2 exf8=N#. 1 … Rg8 2 hxg8=Q/B#. 1 … Rxh7 2 Rxf6#.

1 … Rxe3/g3/h3 2 f5#. 1 … Rxf4 2 Nxf4#. 1 … Rf2/f1 2 exf6#.

64 (from G. Popov, *Thèmes 64*, 1959). Threat 2 Ned8, Nf8, Nc7, Ng7, Nc5, Nxg5, Ned4, Nf4#. 1 … Nc5 2 Nxc5/xg5#. 1 … Qa3+ 2 Nc5#. 1 …Qa1/b2 2 Nc5/xg5/d4, Re3#. 1 … Qc3 2 Nc5/xg5/d4#. 1 … Qd1+/d2+, Rd1+ 2 Ned4#. 1 … Qf4+ 2 Nxf4#. 1 … dxc6 2 Qxc6#. 1 … dxe6 2 Qxe6#. 1 … g4 2 Ned8/f8/c7/g7/c5/g6/d4#. 1 … Bg8 2 Qxg6, Nc5/xg5#. 1 … Bg7 2 Nxg7/c5/xg5#. 1 … Bf8+ 2 Nxf8#.

94

65 (from A. Ellerman, *Observer,* 1920). Threat 2 Qg4#. 1 … Ne5 2 Nh5#. 1 … Qa7+ 2 Nd7#. 1 … Qxf6+ 2 Rf6#. 1 … Qf2/xg1+ 2 Ng4#. 1 … Bf5 2 Qe3#. 1 … Bxf3 2 Be3#. 1 … Kxf3 2 Qg4#.

66 (from E. Goldschmiedt, *Neue Leipziger Zeitung,* 1928). Zugzwang. 1 … Bxb3+ 2 Kxb3#. 1 … Bb1+ 2 Kxb1#. 1 … Rxc7 2 Qxc7#. 1 … Rd8 2 Nxd8#. 1 … Rd6 2 Bd8#. 1 … Rd5 2 exd5#. 1 … Rd4 2 Nxd4#. 1 … Rd3 2 Kxd3#. 1 … Rd2+ 2 Kxd2#. 1 … Rd1 2 Kxd1#.

1 … Nh7/xe6/g6 2 Qxd7#.
1 … Bh4/xf4/f6 2 Rc5#.

67 (from O. Stocchi, *L'Italia Scacchistica*, 1934). Zugzwang.
1 … Kxd5 2 d8=Q/R#. 1 … Kxe3 2 Bg1#. 1 … Bxe3 2 Nf3#.
1 … Bxh4/f4/f6/e7/d8 2 Re4#. 1 … Nf4/e1. 2 Nf5#. 1 … Nxe3 2 Be5#.
1 … Nxh4 2 Rd3#.

68 (from A. R. Gooderson, B. C. P. S. Tourney, 1945). Threat 2 Rd6#.
1 … Rxf6 2 Nec6#. 1 … Bd5+, Re6 2 Q(x)d5#. 1 … Be6 2 Rf4#. 1 … Nd6+
2 Rf3#. 1 … Nxf6+ 2 Bf3#. 1 … Nxg5+/c3+/g3+/d2+/f2+ 2 Rc6#.

69 (from J.M. Rice, McWilliam Tourney, 1956). Threat 2 Qg4#.
1 … Nxd6+ 2 Qf3#. 1 … Nh6+ 2 Nf6#. 1 … Nxh4+ 2 Nf4#.
1 … gxh4 2 Qxh4#. 1 … g4 2 Rh6#.

70 (from K.A.C. Larsen, *Good Companion Folder*, 1920). Threat 2 Qf4#.
1 … Nb6+/d6+/a5+/d2+ 2 Bxc2#. 1 … Ne5+ 2 Nc3#. 1 … d3+ 2 Rxe3#.
1 … e5 2 Nf6#. 1 … Rxd5+ 2 Qxd5#. 1 … Rf5 2 Qxf5#.

71 (from A.F. Ianovcic, *Revista Romana de Sah*, 1933). Threat
2 Nb3#. 1 … Be6 2 Qg7#. 1 … Rd5 2 Qxd5#.
1 … Re6 2 Nf5#. 1 … Rxc1/d3, Bd2

2 Ra(x)d3#. 1 … e6 2 Qg4#.
1 … Rd2 2 Bb2#.

72 (from B. Harley, 1918). Zugzwang. 1 … Nc7/b6.
N(x)b6#. 1 … c3 2 Qd3#. 1 … Bxd7 2 Rxd7#. 1 … Bf5 2 Qc5#.
1 … Bg4 2 Qe4/c5#. 1 … f5 2 Qe5#. 1 … Re2/f1 2 Qd4#. 1 … Rxf3
2 Qxf3/d4#. 1 … g6/g5 2 Ndxf6#. 1 … Rg3/g4/g5/g6/xh2/xg1 2 Rf5#.

73 (from T.R. Dawson, *Vie* 1937). Threat 2 Nf6#. 1 … Raxd5 2 N3c5#.
1 … Qxd5 2 Rc4#. 1 … Bxd3 2 exd3#.1 … Rf5 2 Qf3#. 1 … Rhxd5 2 Qe6#.
1 … Nf2/xg1 2 Qxf4#.

About the Author

Burt Hochberg is the author of *Winning With Chess Psychology* (with Pal Benko), *The 64-Square Looking Glass*, *Chess Braintwisters*, and *Mensa Guide to Chess*. He was the editor of *Chess Life* magazine from 1966–79.